Field Guide to
Nonprofit Program Design,
Marketing and Evaluation

Fourth Edition

By Carter McNamara, MBA, PhD

AUTHENTICITY CONSULTING, LLC
MINNEAPOLIS, MN USA

For reprint permission, more information on Authenticity Consulting, LLC, or to order additional copies of this or any of our other publications, please contact:

>   Authenticity Consulting, LLC
>   4008 Lake Drive Avenue North
>   Minneapolis, MN 55422-1508 USA
>
>   800.971.2250 toll-free
>   763.971.8890 direct
>
>   www.authenticityconsulting.com

Trademarks
Authenticity Circles, Free Management Library, Free Nonprofit Micro-eMBA and Free Micro-eMBA are service marks of Authenticity Consulting, LLC, Minneapolis, Minnesota. "Leveraging the Power of Peers" is a registered mark of Authenticity Consulting, LLC, Minneapolis, Minnesota.

Credits
Cover design by Erin Scott/Wylde Hare Creative, Minneapolis, Minnesota.
Photographs © 2005 JupiterImages Corporation/Comstock.com, primary cover photo;
    © Teri McNamara/ Impressions & Expressions and Erin Scott/Wylde Hare Creative,
    secondary cover photos.
Clip art by Nova Development Corporation Art Explosion 750,000 Images.
Printed by Graphic & Printing Services, Big Lake, Minnesota.

Manufactured in the United States of America
First Edition, June 2002
Second Edition, February 2003
Third Edition, June 2003
Fourth Edition, May 2006
Second printing, December 2007

Waiver of Responsibility
Various Web addresses are referenced in this book. The author and publisher have no legal responsibility or liability for the currency or accuracy of these Web addresses or the content at these addresses.

Publisher's Cataloging in Publication Data
McNamara, Carter, 1953 -
    Field Guide to Nonprofit Program Design, Marketing and Evaluation / by Carter McNamara
    ISBN 1-933719-08-7
    ISBN 978-1-933719-08-5
    1. Nonprofit programs. 2. Marketing. 3. Evaluation. I. Title

Table of Contents

Table of Contents i

Introduction...**vii**
Focus of this Field Guide.. vii
Uses for this Field Guide vii
How to Use Guide vii
Get Help – You Do Not Have to Do It All Yourself x
About the Author xii
About Authenticity Consulting, LLC xii
Acknowledgements...xiii

PART I: BACKGROUND AND PREPARATION **1**

Understanding Nonprofit Organizations and Programs.................**3**
Benefits of Systems View... 3
Understanding "System" of Organizations and Programs............................ 4
System Direction: Mission, Vision, Values, Goals and Strategies................ 8
Nonprofits Programs, Configurations and Types 8
Organization Chart of Typical Start-Up Nonprofit.. 11
Organization Chart of Typical Small Nonprofit with CEO............................ 12
Organization Chart of Typical Medium-to-Large Sized Nonprofit................ 13
Depicting the "System" of a Nonprofit Program... 14
Understanding Life Cycles of Organizations and Programs......................... 16

Understanding General Planning Process....................................**20**
Basic Planning Process and Terms... 20
Guidelines to Ensure Successful Planning and Implementation................... 21
Guidelines for Successful Program Development and Evaluation................. 24

Common Approaches to Program Planning..................................**27**
"Build It and They Will Come" Approach 27
Seat-of-the-Pants Approach.. 28
Incremental Planning Approach 29
Business Planning Approach 29
Business Development Approach 31
Approaches and Good Program Management 32

Strategic Planning: Direction for Programs and Staff **33**
What Is Strategic Planning?.. 33
All Else Flows from Strategic Planning 34
Developing Your Basic Strategic Plan 35

PART II: PROGRAM PLANNING 39

Chronology of Activities in Program Planning 41

Importance of Strong Marketing Orientation 43
Good Marketing Is Good Management 43
Critical Role of Market Research 43

Developing Program Framework 45
Assessment of Community Needs and Interests 45
Vision for Program Participants 48
Desired Outcomes for Program Participants 49
Program Methods to Help Participants Achieve Outcomes 50
Outcomes Goals/Targets and Indicators toward Hitting Targets 52
Outputs/Tangibles Produced by Program Methods 54
Preliminary Program Logic Model 54

Marketing Analysis 56
Target Markets and Their Unique Features 56
Perceived Program Benefits to Each Target Market 58
Packaging 59
Unique Value Proposition 60
Naming and Branding 60
Pricing Analysis 62
Know Your Competition 63
What Current or Potential Collaborators Exist? 64
Applicable Laws and Regulations 65
Intellectual Property – Copyrights, Trademarks and Patents 65
Summary Description of Programs and Service 66
Remaining Marketing Analysis Tasks and Considerations 66
Marketing Goals 66

Planning Program Development 68
Guidelines about Estimating Costs 68
Starting Your Program 71

Planning Program Operations 73
Advertising and Promotions 73
Sales 74
Customer Service 75
Delivery of Services 76
Personnel Management 77
Materials (Supplies, Tools, Equipment and Facilities) 78

Planning Finances to Operate Program 80
Key Financial Concepts 80
How to Develop Summary Program Budget 81
Sample Summary Program Budget Format 87

PART III: PROGRAM EVALUATION..89

Understanding Program Evaluation 91
Myths about Program Evaluation 91
What Is Program Evaluation? 92
Reasons to Do Program Evaluation 92
Basic Ingredients for Program Evaluation 93
Major Considerations to Designing Your Program Evaluation 94

Common Types of Program Evaluations 96
Implementation Evaluation – What Are We Doing? 96
Process Evaluation – How Does the Program Work? 97
Goals-Based Evaluation – Are We Achieving Goals? 98
Outcomes Evaluation – What Are Impacts on Clients? 100

Planning Your Program Evaluation 102
Should You Hire a Program Evaluator? 102
Who Is the Audience for Your Program Evaluation? 103
What Management Decisions Do You Need to Make? 103
What Evaluation Questions Should You Answer? 105
What Information Is Needed to Answer Evaluation Questions? 106
What Are Best Sources for This Information/Data? 106
What Are Best Methods to Collect Information/Data? 107
How Will You Analyze and Interpret Your Results? 109
How Will You Report Your Evaluation Results? 110
Who Should Conduct the Evaluation? 111
Review and Test Evaluation Plans...111
Ethics and Information Privacy 112
Pitfalls to Avoid During Evaluation Planning 112

PART IV: ASSEMBLING AND IMPLEMENTING PLANS..............115

Role of Leadership 117

Assembling Plans...118
Sections Common to Many Plan Documents 118
Assembling Program Development Plan.....................................120
Assembling Program Marketing Plan..121
Assembling Program Promotions Plans (Sales, Advertising and Promotions) 122
Assembling Program Operations Plan...123
Assembling Program Staffing Plan 124
Assembling Nonprofit Business Plan 125
Assembling Program Evaluation Plan 129
Assembling Fundraising Proposal 130
Have Plans Reviewed By Others..133
Approve Final Version of Plans 134

Implementing Plans 135
Tools to Track Status of Implementation 135
Capture Learnings from Implementation of Plans... 136

APPENDICES.. 137

Appendix A: Key Terms.. 139

Appendix B: Resources for Nonprofits..................................... 143
Free Management Library^{SM} 143
Free Nonprofit Micro-eMBA^{SM} Organization Development Program...................... 144
Organizations Assisting Nonprofits.. 145
Free, On-Line Newsletters and Forums.. 146

Appendix C: Checklist of Nonprofit Management Indicators 147

Appendix D: Worksheets... 161
Assessment of Community Needs and Interests... 163
Vision for Program Participants 166
Desired Outcomes for Program Participants 168
Methods to Help Participants Achieve Desired Outcomes................................... 170
Outcomes Goals/Targets and Indicators toward Hitting Targets.......................... 172
Preliminary Program Logic Model... 173
Target Markets, Their Features and Benefits They Perceive 174
Packaging Analysis 175
Unique Value Proposition Description.. 176
Program Name Analysis.. 177
Pricing Analysis.. 178
Competitor Analysis.. 180
Collaborator Analysis 182
Laws and Regulations... 183
Description of Service 185
Summary of Remaining Marketing Analysis Tasks and Considerations 187
Marketing Goals 188
Program Planning Development.. 189
Advertising and Promotions 193
Sales Planning 194
Customer Service Planning 195
Delivery of Services 196
Personnel Needs 200
Materials (Supplies, Tools, Equipment and Facilities).. 203
Summary Program Budget 206
Planning Your Program Evaluation... 210

Appendix E: Basic Methods in Business Research.............215

Planning Your Business Research 215
Overview of Methods to Collect Information.. 217
Ethics: Information Release from Research Participants........................... 219
Guidelines to Conducting Observations 220
Guidelines to Writing Questionnaires... 222
Guidelines to Conducting Interviews 225
Guidelines to Conducting Focus Groups... 229
Guidelines to Completing Case Studies.. 231
Guidelines to Conducting Pilot Research (Test Market) 231
Convenient Methods to Collect Information 233
Major Sources of Trends Information about Nonprofits 234
Major Sources of Market Research Information 234
Analyzing and Interpreting Research Data.. 236

Appendix F: Major Methods of Advertising and Promotions.....237

Collateral, Advertising and Outreach 237
Promotional Activities through the Media... 240
Other Promotional Activities and Events 241

Recommended Readings – an Annotated List 243

Index 249

Introduction

Focus of this Field Guide

To effectively design a program, you must have clear understanding of the program's clients and their needs to be met by the program. That understanding comes from conducting an effective marketing analysis. To effectively advertise and promote a program, you must have clear understanding of the program's clients, their needs and their habits, along with the benefits of the program to the clients. To effectively evaluate a program, you must have clear understanding of the program's goals and intended outcomes, and integrate indicators of success into the program's design well before the program even starts operating.

Thus, the activities of program design, marketing and evaluation are highly integrated and should be treated as such. This Field Guide provides clear, concise, comprehensive and highly practical guidelines for all critical aspects of designing, marketing and evaluating a nonprofit program "from the ground up." The guidelines can also be used to analyze and improve the design, marketing and evaluation of already established programs.

The guide includes occasional references to USA-specific and Canadian-specific information, and on those occasions, the information is marked as such.

Uses for this Field Guide

You can use this Field Guide:

1.   During, or shortly after, strategic planning to evolve new strategic goals and strategies into new, well-developed programs.

2.   To redesign and refocus current programs to be more closely aligned with current strategic goals and strategies.

3.   To reposition current programs according to results of detailed market planning.

4.   To evaluate program performance against goals and outcomes.

5.   To analyze program effectiveness and efficiencies in delivering services to clients.

6.   To help analyze current resources (staffing, supplies, tools, facilities, equipment, etc.), including their levels, focus and performance toward achieving strategic goals.

How to Use Guide

You need not have any previous knowledge about nonprofit program design, marketing and/or evaluation to benefit from this Field Guide. Guidelines are written in an easy-to-understand and "how to" fashion that you can implement right away.

The format of the guide is designed so each section readily flows into the next, allowing you to progress through the guide from cover to cover, step-by-step to design, market and evaluate your nonprofit program. The general flow of the guide is:

1.   PART I sets the stage for your program planning and evaluation by conveying the overall "territory" of a nonprofit program.

2.   PART II helps you to design your program, including starting the program and operating the program. You will collect your thoughts on various worksheets that are referenced from each section in PART II.

3.   PART III helps you to design a careful approach to evaluate your program, either at some point in the future or right now if you have been operating your program for a while. You will also collect your thoughts on various worksheets.

4.   PART IV helps you to organize all of the useful information that you collected on the various worksheets and assemble them into any of a variety of useful plans that you might want for your program. This part also helps you to ensure that you actually implement the various plans and learn a lot at the same time.

As with any resource, people benefit most if they actually apply it to a real-world situation. Therefore, you are advised to use the Field Guide to actually design, market and evaluate a nonprofit program.

You can use this Field Guide according to any of the following approaches:

1.   Read it from cover to cover to quickly get clear perspective on what is required to design, market and evaluate a program.

2.   Implement the guidelines from cover to cover to build a program "from the ground up."

3.   Read PART II, PART III and then PART IV to generate a fundraising proposal or business plan, each with well-designed approaches to evaluation.

4.   Read PART II and PART IV to generate a marketing plan, including sales, advertising and promotions plans.

5.   Read PART III and then PART IV to design and implement an evaluation plan for an already established program.

Note that you will best benefit from this Field Guide if your nonprofit organization conducts strategic planning on a regular basis. If it does not, you should consider starting strategic planning as soon as possible.

 In this Field Guide, the section, "Developing Your Basic Strategic Plan," in PART I, provides a starting point for you.

 Also, see the annotated list of resources about strategic planning on page 247.

Formats Used to Reference and Organize Information

References to other content within the Field Guide, other related sections that you may want to look at more closely.

References to other content in external resources, such as other books.

References to content available on the web, such as tools and sample documents.

Opportunities to complete sections of the worksheets provided on the Web or in the Appendices.

1. Numbered lists suggest guidelines and the order in which they should be applied. They also indicate that there are a certain number of items of a particular type.

   ■ Bulleted lists provide information that can be considered in any order and may not be all-inclusive.

Use of Terms

This guide regularly refers to certain terms that can have various meanings and applications, depending on the context in which the terms are used. A glossary is in Appendix A. However, there are two pairs of terms to consider in particular.

Clients and Customers

The guide refers to "clients" as the people who benefit from the services of a nonprofit. If you prefer, you might think of clients as "customers". Clients might be:

- Attendees to an art show

- Buyers of an item sold by the nonprofit

- Citizens attending a civic event

- Grantees of a foundation

- Members of a congregation

- Members of an association

- Participants in social service programs

- Patients in a hospital

- Patrons to a library

- Students in a school

Products and Services

The author believes that any value provided by a nonprofit to the community is ultimately a service to the community. Therefore, this Field Guide refers to products and services as "services," although the guide certainly is relevant to tangible "products," as well. If you prefer, you can interchange the two terms when reading this Field Guide.

Worksheets to Copy or Download

This guide includes numerous worksheets that planners can use to collect and organize the results from their planning activities. If the formats of the worksheets seem useful, the owner of the Field Guide can make copies of the worksheets for use within their organization. Consultants may duplicate the worksheets for use with their clients, as long as the client organization owns at least one copy of the Field Guide. Worksheets can also be customized, with appropriate attribution to this author.

To download a copy of the worksheets:

1. Point your Web browser to the Web address:
   http://www.authenticityconsulting.com/pubs/PG_gdes/worksheets.doc
   NOTE: It might take a couple of minutes to download this file.

2. Save the document to your computer's disk, for example, use the "Save As" command in your browser and name the file "worksheets".

Get Help – You Do Not Have to Do It All Yourself

Many Free Resources Are Available to You

Whether you are planning your program's development or evaluation, you do not have to do it all yourself. There are several sources of help available to you. Start getting to know them now so you will be able to fully use them by the time you start your planning activities.

 Appendix B includes an extensive list of resources, many of them free. Take a minute to glance through that list, including reviewing the following items.

1. **Free Management Library**^{SM}
   Authenticity Consulting, LLC, provides this Library, one of the world's largest collections of well-organized free resources about personal, professional and organizational development.

2. **Free Nonprofit Micro-eMBA^{SM} Organization Development Program**
    Authenticity Consulting, LLC, also provides this on-line, self-directed program to start and manage a nonprofit organization. The program includes 12 learning modules, each with free reading materials, study questions and guidelines to apply materials from the modules.

3. **Organizations Assisting Nonprofits**
    There are several that you can choose from if you want to recruit a volunteer or hire a consultant to help you. You can probably conduct many of the activities in this Field Guide with the help of your program staff and, hopefully, some members of the Board. You might need a consultant at some point. You can "cross that bridge when you come to it.".

4. **Free, On-Line Newsletters**
    Sign up for at least three of these newsletters. You will find valuable, free information from experts in the field of nonprofit management. Be sure to sign up for the CharityChannel's forums – there are several to choose from.

Use Board Committees or Task Forces

One of the primary responsibilities of a Board of Directors is to set the strategic direction for the organization and ensure that the organization follows that direction. The Board carries out this responsibility by overseeing the development and implementation of a variety of plans. The Board often oversees plans through use of committees or task forces, depending on the nature and needs of the Board. For example:

1. **Board Planning Committee**
    Often oversees development and implementation of the strategic plan. This committee might be comprised of officers of the Board and/or Chairs of the various committees or all of the members of the Board.

2. **Board Programs Committee**
    Can be very helpful during program planning and implementation, particularly while developing the top-level, conceptual layout (logic) model of the program and also during operations planning. This committee is often charged to oversee program evaluation activities, as well.

3. **Board Marketing Committee**
    Can be very helpful as you conduct your marketing analysis, and especially while planning advertising and promotions.

4. **Board Finance Committee**
    Can be very helpful as you organize and report financial information on the planning and operations of your program.

Remember that a nonprofit corporation is a public trust and the public expects the Board of Directors to take full responsibility for the ongoing governance of the nonprofit. Therefore, the nonprofit – and the public – can expect the Board to play a strong role in planning the program's development and evaluation.

 For more information about Boards of Directors, see the annotated list of resources on page 243.

About the Author

Carter McNamara, MBA, PhD, is a partner in Authenticity Consulting, LLC. He has strong real-world experience in leadership and supervision from working his way along the "ladder" from individual contributor to director. He has led and managed in a variety of types of organizations, including startup, large for-profit corporation, nonprofit, public-private, hospital and university.

He consults in a wide array of services to for-profit and nonprofit organizations. He has extensive experience in organizational and management development, including focus on program development and evaluation. He is also the author of *Field Guide to Developing and Operating Your Nonprofit Board of Directors, Field Guide to Nonprofit Strategic Planning and Facilitation, Field Guide to Leadership and Supervision for Nonprofit Staff* and *Field Guide to Consulting and Organizational Development With Nonprofits.*

He is founder and developer of the Authenticity Circles^{SM} and Leaders Circles® peer coaching group programs, Free Management Library^{SM}, Free Micro-eMBA^{SM} and Nonprofit Micro-MBA^{SM}. He has extensive training and experience in training and coaching, including Action Learning and peer coaching groups. He is confident of the ability of learners to recognize their own development needs and direct their own learning.

Dr. McNamara holds a BA in Social and Behavioral Sciences, a BS in Computer Science, an MBA from the University of St. Thomas in Minneapolis, Minnesota, and a PhD in Human and Organization Development from The Union Institute in Cincinnati, Ohio.

About Authenticity Consulting, LLC

Authenticity Consulting, LLC, publisher of this Field Guide, is a consulting firm specializing in development of nonprofit organizations, management and programs. While many firms specialize in one or a few specific services to nonprofits, Authenticity brings a highly comprehensive and integrated approach to building the capacity of the entire organization.

Authenticity Consulting provides consultation, training and publications in the areas of:

- Board Development and Governance
- Strategic Planning and Facilitation
- Nonprofit Business Development (social entrepreneurship)
- Program Design, Marketing and Evaluation
- Leadership and Management Development

The firm also provides powerful, practical peer coaching group programs for networking, training, problem solving and support – either free-standing or to enrich other programs – through the Authenticity Circles and Leaders Circles peer coaching group model. Their unique Action Learning-based group coaching process ensures ongoing support and accountability among participants. They also offer ongoing, one-on-one coaching sessions with key leaders in client organizations.

Authenticity Consulting can be reached at 800-971-2250 or at http://www.authenticityconsulting.com/ on the Web for additional information.

Acknowledgements

This Field Guide would not have been possible without the ongoing contributions of my business partners, Theresa McNamara and Andrew Horsnell. Theresa is a partner in Authenticity Consulting, LLC, and is also my partner in life. She has extensive, real-world skills in planning and marketing, and is a consistent task master to ensure the highest quality in all of our publications. Andy contributed greatly to this Field Guide, as well. Andy has the amazing ability to make complex matters, like marketing and financial management, seem quite simple. Andy is an expert in many facets of nonprofit development, including business development and business planning. His expertise is threaded throughout this Field Guide.

PART I:

BACKGROUND AND

PREPARATION

Understanding Nonprofit Organizations and Programs

It would be very difficult to design a garden without first having a good sense about how large the garden should be, what plants grow best next to each other, which ones grow the tallest, which ones should be harvested first, etc. That principle is true for planning and evaluating nonprofit programs, as well. To effectively plan or evaluate a nonprofit program, it is very important to have a coherent understanding of the overall "territory" of the nonprofit organization and its various programs. It is quite difficult, if not impossible, to build something without at least basic knowledge of its parts and how those parts fit together. One of the most effective ways to learn to understand complex concepts, such as organizations and programs, is by adopting a systems view. A systems view helps people to see the major parts and how those parts work together. That is why many training programs about organizations, management and business start out by explaining this systems view to its learners.

Benefits of Systems View

1. **More effective planning**
   The planning process is basically working one's way backwards through the system of a program, including identifying its desired results (vision, goals and outcomes), what outputs (tangibles) will indicate that those results have been achieved, what processes will produce those outputs, and what inputs are required to conduct those processes in the system.

2. **More effective evaluation of programs**
   Nonprofit experts remind us that the success of a program is determined primarily by the quality of the benefits (outcomes) to clients who participated in the program, not only from the number of clients (outputs) who participated in the program. Consequently, outcomes evaluation has become a major topic in nonprofit organization development. This form of evaluation requires careful analysis of the system of a program.

3. **More effective leadership**
   The most important responsibilities of a leader are to set direction and influence others to follow that direction. It is difficult to establish direction for a program and to keep that program on its course if you do not understand how the program works in the first place. Without a clear understanding of the overall nature and needs of a program, the leader can get lost in the day-to-day activities of the program, never really giving attention to the more important activities, such as planning the program's overall direction and organizing the program's resources. As a result, the leader "cannot see the forest for the trees." The leader ends up working harder, rather than smarter.

4. **More effective communications**
   From this Field Guide, you will learn that one of the most important ingredients for the success of any system, including for a nonprofit organization and its programs, is ongoing communications among all the parts of the system. Some of the first symptoms of a program in trouble are sporadic and insufficient communications. In these situations, members of the program staff often struggle to see beyond their own roles in the organization. Consequently, the program is much less effective than it could be otherwise. Without a clear understanding of the parts of a program and how they relate to each other, it is difficult to know what to communicate and to whom in the overall organization.

5. **More effective problem solving**

 To effectively solve problems in organizations and programs, it is critical to be able to identify the real causes of the problems and how to address those causes. Without clear understanding of the "big picture" of an organization or program, nonprofit leaders focus only on the behaviors and events associated with the program, rather than on the systems and structures that caused the problems to occur in the first place.

6. **More effective overall organizational development**

 The most effective forms of organizational development result from use of a variety of development strategies. These strategies can include strategic planning, program development, management and leadership development, team building, supervisory development, performance management (of organizations, groups and employees), and principles of organizational change. Any leader would be hard-pressed to employ these various strategies in an effective fashion without a good understanding of the overall systems of their organizations, programs, groups and employees. Consequently, having a systems view is critical to accomplishing effective organizational development.

7. **Avoiding Founder's Syndrome**

 Founder's Syndrome occurs when an organization or program operates primarily according to the personality of one of the members of the organization (usually the founder), rather than to its mission (purpose). When first starting their organizations or programs, founders often have to do whatever it takes to get the organizations off the ground, including making seat-of-the-pants decisions to deal with frequent crises that suddenly arise. As a result, founders often struggle to see the larger picture and to make more proactive decisions. Consequently, their organizations get stuck in a highly reactive mode characterized by lack of funds and having to deal with one major crisis after another. One of the best "cures" for this syndrome is for the nonprofit leaders to gain broader understanding of the structures and processes of an organization and also an appreciation for the importance of planning.

Understanding "System" of Organizations and Programs

Organizations and programs are systems. Simply put, a system is an organized collection of parts that are highly integrated to accomplish an overall goal. The system has various inputs that go through certain processes to produce certain outputs that, together, accomplish the overall desired goal for the system. A highly functioning system continually exchanges feedback among its various parts to ensure that they remain closely aligned and focused on achieving the overall goal of the system. A system is usually made up of many smaller systems. For example, a nonprofit organization is made up of programs, groups and people.

Let's look more closely at the important aspects of a system, including your nonprofit organization or program.

1. **Inputs**

 are items that are used by the various processes in the system to achieve the overall goal of the system. Types of inputs are people, money, equipment, facilities, supplies, people's ideas, people's time, etc. For example, the inputs to a nonprofit program that provides training to clients might include trained teachers, clients, training materials, classrooms, funding, and paper and pencils. Inputs can also be major forces that influence the organization and its programs. For example, various laws and regulations influence how the program is operated. Inputs are often identified with the costs to obtain and use them.

Simply put, a program's budget is a listing of the program's costs (expenses), and monies that are expected to be earned or raised (revenues).

2. **Processes**
   are series of activities conducted by the system to manipulate its various inputs to achieve the overall desired goal of the system. For example, the major processes used by a nonprofit program that provides training to clients might include recruitment of clients, pre-testing, training, post-testing and certification. Processes can range from putting a piece of paper on a desk to manufacturing a space shuttle. Nonprofit leaders are usually concerned with the most important, recurring processes in the organization, for example, its plans, programs, policies and procedures.

   Some nonprofit experts, especially fundraisers, often refer to the processes as the program "activities," "methods," or "throughputs."

3. **Outputs**
   are the tangible results produced by the system. Outputs are often described by using numbers, for example, the number of clients who completed a certain program. Outputs are often mistaken to indicate the success of an organization or one of its programs. For example, nonprofit leaders might mistakenly assume that because a program served a large number of clients, the program must have been very successful. That is not a valid assumption. The success of a nonprofit organization or program is determined, not by the range and number of clients trained (the program's outputs), but by how the clients benefited (the program's outcomes).

4. **Outcomes**
   are the impacts on the people affected by the system, for example, on the clients served by a program. Outcomes are usually specified in terms of changed:

   a) Knowledge (short-term outcomes)

   b) Behaviors, especially those that comprise useful skills (intermediate outcomes)

   c) Attitudes, values, conditions, such as increased security, stability, pride, etc.
      (long-term outcomes)

   Some examples of outcomes from a program are that clients accomplish the ability to read, live alone or drive a car. Notice the major difference between outputs (measures of the organization's activities) and outcomes (measures of the clients' changes as a result of participating in the organization's activities).

5. **Feedback**
   is continuously exchanged among the various parts of the system. Feedback comes from a variety of sources in the organization, including communications among Board members, the Chief Executive Officer, other staff, clients and others in the community. Feedback can also come from evaluation of the organization, programs and personnel. This ongoing feedback, or communications, is absolutely critical to the success of the organization and its programs. That is why, to be a highly effective nonprofit leader, you have to continually be communicating with others in your organization.

6. **Goals**

    are the ultimate results that the system wants to accomplish. All systems are goal-directed. For example, plants, animals and people strive to stay alive and to replicate themselves. Nonprofit organizations and programs must have clear goals, as well. That is why it is very important for leaders to establish goals and effectively communicate them throughout the organization. The overall goals of the nonprofit organization are usually described in terms of its mission, or purpose. In addition, many nonprofits often associate a vision, or clear depiction, of what the nonprofit and its clients will look like when working successfully at some point in the future. The mission, vision and strategic goals are usually determined during strategic planning. Thus, strategic planning is a very important responsibility of the nonprofit leader.

    Note that an organization can have goals in a variety of dimensions, for example, goals regarding activities of the organization, activities of clients or impacts on clients.

 To learn more about systems, see the annotated list of resources on page 247.

The graphic on the following page depicts the overall system of a nonprofit organization.

Major Parts and Processes in "System" of Nonprofit Organization

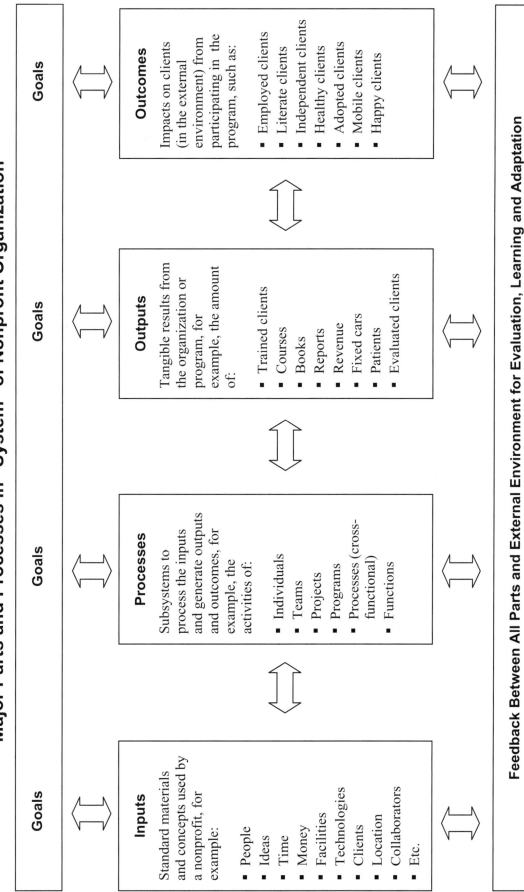

Inputs

Standard materials and concepts used by a nonprofit, for example:

- People
- Ideas
- Time
- Money
- Facilities
- Technologies
- Clients
- Location
- Collaborators
- Etc.

Processes

Subsystems to process the inputs and generate outputs and outcomes, for example, the activities of:

- Individuals
- Teams
- Projects
- Programs
- Processes (cross-functional)
- Functions

Outputs

Tangible results from the organization or program, for example, the amount of:

- Trained clients
- Courses
- Books
- Reports
- Revenue
- Fixed cars
- Patients
- Evaluated clients

Outcomes

Impacts on clients (in the external environment) from participating in the program, such as:

- Employed clients
- Literate clients
- Independent clients
- Healthy clients
- Adopted clients
- Mobile clients
- Happy clients

Goals   Goals   Goals   Goals

Feedback Between All Parts and External Environment for Evaluation, Learning and Adaptation

Feedback from the environment is especially from standard inputs, environmental scanning, market research and program evaluations. Feedback to the environment is especially from outputs, public relations, advertising and promotions, and outcomes.

System Direction: Mission, Vision, Values, Goals and Strategies

All systems have a purpose, or mission, in their life. They also have certain methods, or strategies, to work toward that mission. For example, think of people you know who have complained that they do not feel meaning in their lives. Often, it is because they are not in touch with their purpose or mission. Usually, when people discover their mission in life, they feel much more fulfilled in their lives and work. They may even develop a clear vision of what they want to be by a certain time in the future. They might identify certain overall priorities, or values, in how they want to work and live.

Some people prefer to set goals along the way while working toward their vision, for example, goals to finish college, have a family and establish a career. They often set about to find ways, or strategies, to achieve their goals, for example, enroll in college, start dating and get career counseling. They may set timelines for achieving their vision and their goals. After they have set timelines, they think about what resources they will need, for example, money, house and training.

Other systems are quite similar, including nonprofit organizations and programs. To be effective, they need to be clear about their mission, or purpose. They should establish clear goals and strategies along the way while working toward their mission.

Organizations establish the mission, goals and strategies during the strategic planning process. To be effective, the strategic planning process must include action plans that specify who will do what and by when to implement the various strategies. The process must also include timelines for completion of goals and a list of resources needed to implement the strategies. The list of resources often includes a budget, or list of what funding is needed and how it will be spent.

 We will review more about the strategic planning process in an upcoming section, "Strategic Planning: Direction for Programs and Staff."

Nonprofits Programs, Configurations and Types

It is important for program developers and evaluators to have some sense about what a nonprofit program really is. That sentence might sound too obvious to include in this Field Guide, but it is surprising, for example, how many nonprofit personnel set out to evaluate a program when they do not even really have a program to evaluate!

Discerning Programs from Activities

Activities

Activities are a set of events that, although they are or seem beneficial to the community, are so loosely or informally conducted that it is difficult to readily ascertain if the events are truly needed by the community and/or are making any substantive difference in the community.

There are many types of activities that can be useful to a community, even someone standing on a corner and handing out food to whomever happens to walk by. On first impression, that event might seem beneficial to the community. However, without knowing whether the food is safe, whether those walking by really need the food or not, or whether handing out the food on the corner is the best means to provide the food, it is difficult to ascertain whether the event deserves the ongoing investment of resources from the community.

Programs

A nonprofit program is an integrated set of services conducted to meet specific, verified community need(s) by achieving certain specific outcomes among specific group(s) of clients in that community. Services include ongoing systematic evaluations, as much as possible, to ensure that the specific outcomes are indeed being achieved and that the community's resources are best invested in that particular program.

The community need and the services to meet that need are verified by more than anecdotal evidence – by using credible, valid means of research to collect information and make conclusions. Information is collected from primary sources (those persons in need, community leaders, etc.) and, as much as possible, from secondary sources (census data, other established program models, etc.).

The research and conclusions together suggest a concise, systematic "theory of action" or "chain of events" that, in turn, suggests and explains why the new program will work – or how the established program works as it does. The theory of action may require program personnel to specifically define and/or set parameters around certain key terms, for example, "leadership" or "youth."

In essence, a well-designed program is similar to a well-designed research project from which a community can benefit and a great deal can be learned. Common examples of nonprofit programs are food-shelf programs, transportation programs, training programs, health services programs and arts programs.

Nonprofits often define their programs during strategic planning. Programs become major methods, or strategies, to reach strategic goals. For example, a nonprofit might have a mission to "Enhance the quality of life for young adults by promoting literacy." Major strategies, or programs, to work toward that mission might be a High School Equivalency Training Program and a Transportation Program to get the young adults to the Training Program.

The typical nonprofit organizational structure is built around programs. Two other major aspects of the nonprofit structure are its governance (the Board and, for some, the Chief Executive Officer) and its central administration. The Board oversees the entire nonprofit organization. The central administration exists to use the nonprofit's common resources primarily to ensure each program is developed and operated effectively.

Program Configurations

Programs have two major types of configurations, including:

1. Free-standing program, where the program's services are delivered completely within the context of the program.

2. Multi-program effort, where two or more programs are tightly integrated to provide a common set of services to meet one, major unmet need in the community.

The organizations that provide programs can be:

- Free-standing, where a program, or multi-program effort, is provided completely within the context of one organization.

- Multi-organization (or collaborative) effort, where a program, or integration of programs, is provided by two or more organizations that work closely together to meet a major, unmet need in the community.

Types of Program Results

There are a variety of major types of program results. They are usually packaged as 1) services that provide intangible results to clients, and/or 2) products that provide tangible results to clients.

There are a wide variety of types of program services and products, for example, in the categories of:

- Advocacy and lobbying

- Arts

- Associations (business leagues, labor organizations, social clubs, associations of specific types of professions, etc.)

- Civic or community services

- Foundations

- Hospitals

- Literary

- Religious

- Schools

- Scientific

- Social services

- Others?

Organization Chart of Typical Start-Up Nonprofit

It is common that a start-up nonprofit organization has one major program carried out by a hands-on group of volunteers, some of whom act as the Board of Directors and others who act as staff. Both groups might be involved in providing services to clients. A new nonprofit often does not include the role of Chief Executive Officer.

Note that there is no certain standard that suggests whether a nonprofit is categorized as small, medium or large in size. However, conventionally, small nonprofits usually have no paid staff or only one or two programs.

Also, note that the charts on this and the following pages are functional in design. Functional design of organizations is based on a top-down hierarchy of positions. Certainly, there are other designs of nonprofit organizations that do not follow this design. For example, self-organizing organizations might have different forms at various times, depending on the strategic priorities and culture of the organization.

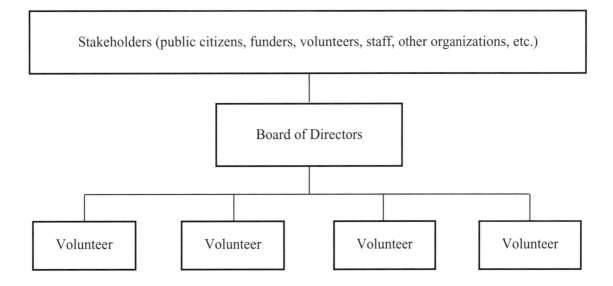

Organization Chart of Typical Small Nonprofit with CEO

A nonprofit might have a part-time or full-time Chief Executive Officer (CEO) in a paid or volunteer position. If the nonprofit has staff in addition to the CEO, the CEO supervises the other staff members, who also might be part-time or full-time, and occupy paid or volunteer positions. The CEO reports to a Board of Directors comprised of volunteers, and the Board members supervise the CEO.

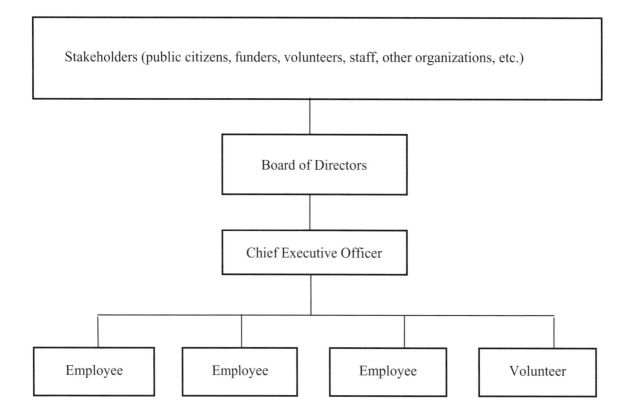

Organization Chart of Typical Medium-to-Large Sized Nonprofit

An organization like this usually has a paid Chief Executive Officer, often on a full-time basis, who supervises various staff members, again who might be paid on a full-time or part-time basis. Staff might also include volunteers. The Chief Executive Officer reports to a Board of Directors comprised of volunteers, and the Board supervises the CEO. This nonprofit often has more than one program, is managed by employees, and is staffed by employees or volunteers.

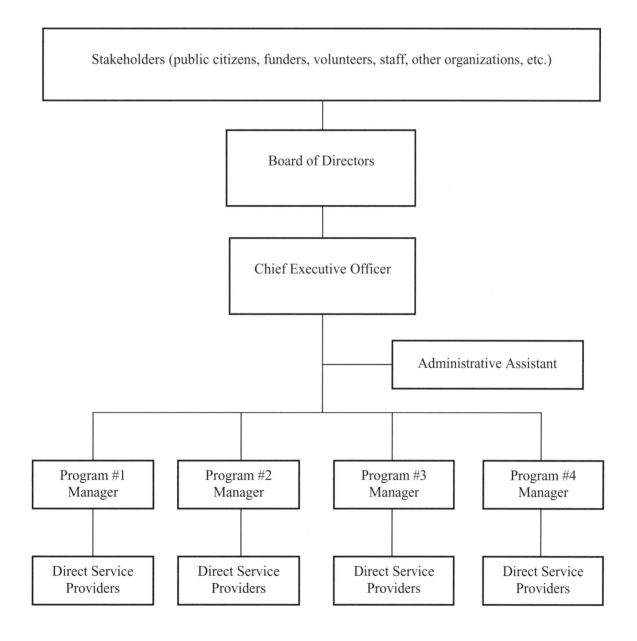

Depicting the "System" of a Nonprofit Program

In the previous section, we discussed how to understand and portray the system of any organization or program. We mentioned the major aspects of systems, including their inputs, processes, outputs, outcomes and feedback. We mentioned that, in a healthy system, all of these aspects are aligned to achieve the overall goals of the system. Programs are systems so they have these aspects of systems, too.

One of the best ways to get a clear picture of the system of a program is to develop a logic model. A logic model is a top-level depiction of the inputs, processes, outputs and outcomes of a program. Constructing a logic model helps program planners and evaluators answer the following questions:

- What outcomes does the program want to help its participants to achieve, including short-term, intermediate and long-term outcomes?

- What activities, or processes, need to occur in the program for those outcomes to be achieved?

- What resources are needed to be able to conduct the processes?

PART II of this Field Guide includes guidelines to design a logic model for your own program.

Example of Logic Model for Nonprofit Program
"Self-Directed Learning Center (SDLC)"

The following example is intended to portray the scope and level of detail in a program's logic model. The model depicts a fictional program called the Self-Directed Learning Center (SDLC). The mission, or purpose, of the program is to enhance the quality of life for low-income adults by providing free, on-line training materials and programs and by helping them help each other to learn. Feedback from the environment is from inputs, environmental scanning, market research and program evaluations. Feedback to the environment is principally from public relations, advertising and promotions, outputs and outcomes.

Inputs	Processes	Outputs	Short-Term Outcomes	Intermediate Outcomes	Long-Term Outcomes
▪ Collaborators	▪ Provide peer-assistance models in which learners support each other	▪ 30 groups that used peer models	▪ High-school diploma for graduates	▪ Full-time employment for learners in jobs that require high-school education	▪ Improved attitude toward self and society for graduates
▪ Computers		▪ 100 finished training programs	▪ Increased likelihood and interest for learners to attend advanced schooling		▪ Improved family life for families of graduates
▪ Free articles and other publications on the Web	▪ Provide free, on-line training program: Basics of Self-Directed Learning	▪ 900 learners who finished Basics of Self-Directed Learning		▪ Independent living for learners from using salary to rent housing	▪ Increased reliability and improved judgment of learners
▪ Funders					
▪ Self-directed learners	▪ Provide free, on-line training program: Basic Life Skills	▪ 900 learners who finished Basic Life Skills		▪ Strong basic life skills for learners	
▪ Supplies					
▪ Volunteers	▪ Provide free, on-line training program: Passing Your GED Exam	▪ 900 learners who finished Passing Your GED Exam			
▪ Web					

15

Understanding Life Cycles of Organizations and Programs

What Are Life Cycles? Why Is It Important to Understand Them?

Organizations and programs go through different life cycles just as people do. For example, people go through infancy and childhood phases characterized by lots of rapid growth. People in these phases often do whatever it takes just to stay alive, for example, eating, seeking shelter and sleeping. Often, these people make impulsive, highly reactive decisions based on whatever is going on around them now.

Start-up organizations and programs are like this, too. Often, founders of the organizations or programs and their various members have to do whatever is necessary just to stay in business. Leaders in these situations often make highly reactive, seat-of-the-pants decisions. They fear that taking the time to slow down and do planning means time away from dealing with the latest crisis.

In our comparison of organizations and programs to people, we note that, as people continue to mature, they begin to understand more about the world and themselves. Over time, they develop a certain kind of wisdom that sees them through many of the challenges in their lives and work. They learn to plan and to use a certain amount of discipline to implement those plans. Basically, they learn to effectively lead and manage themselves.

To survive well into the future, organizations and programs must be led and managed effectively, as well. Experienced leaders have learned to recognize the current life cycle of an organization or program. These leaders understand the types of problems faced by the organization or program during that life cycle. That understanding gives them perspective and helps them to effectively respond to decisions and problems in the workplace.

One Perspective on Life Cycles

The following useful table is summarized from Richard L. Daft's work and book, *Organizational Theory and Design* (West Publishing, St. Paul, Minnesota, 1992), which, in turn, is based on information from Robert E. Quinn and Kim Cameron's *Organizational Life Cycles and Some Shifting Criteria of Effectiveness,* Management Science, 29, (Institute for Operations Research and the Management Sciences, 1983), pp. 31-51.

Remember that the following information is about life cycles of systems, and systems include organizations, programs and even you and your job.

Life Cycles of Organizations and Programs

Aspects	Birth	Youth	Midlife	Maturity
Size	Small	Medium	Large	Very large
Bureaucratic	Non-bureaucratic	Pre-bureaucratic	Bureaucratic	Very bureaucratic
Division of labor	Overlapping tasks	Some departments	Many departments	Extensive, with small jobs and many descriptions
Centralization	One-person rule	Two leaders rule	Two department heads	Top-management heavy
Formalization	No written rules	Few rules	Policy and procedures manuals	Extensive
Administrative intensity	Secretary, no professional staff	Increasing clerical and maintenance	Increasing professional and staff support	Large– multiple departments
Internal systems	Nonexistent	Crude budget and information system	Control systems in place: budget, performance, reports, etc.	Extensive – planning, financial and personnel added
Lateral teams for coordination	None	Top leaders only	Some use of task forces	Frequent at lower levels

Another Perspective on Life Cycles

This author often views life cycles in the following phases (rather than stages). As with any life cycles, they are highly integrated and not always sequential in order. The phases include infancy, growth and maturity. Decline, stagnation or growth can occur between the infancy, growth and maturity phases. This simple approach to life cycles is straightforward to describe to clients and easy for clients to apply on their own.

Infancy Phase	Growth Phase	Maturity Phase
▪ Clarify mission, vision and values	▪ Focus on effectiveness of services	▪ Sustain momentum
▪ Firm up the leadership systems, including Board and CEO role	▪ Focus on efficiencies through policies and procedures	▪ Focus on innovation
▪ Clarify clients and stakeholders	▪ Expand services, especially current services to new clients	▪ Cultivate renewal
▪ Clarify desired outcomes from services	▪ Accomplish fundraising streams for increased sustainability	▪ Focus on succession planning and risk management
▪ Clarify methods to deliver services	▪ Document successful operations	▪ Diversify resources, including funding
▪ Build image in community	▪ Attend to longer-range planning	▪ Share learning with other people and organizations
▪ Build infrastructure and lay groundwork for future sustainability	▪ Implement and polish plans	▪ Expand services, especially new services to new clients
	▪ Expand evaluations and accountabilities, and capture learnings	▪ Seek to successfully duplicate model elsewhere
	▪ Systematize major functions, including systematic plans	▪ Attend to even longer-range planning
		▪ Manage change and transformation

Consider Life Cycles in Your Organization

Think about the traits associated with life cycles in the table, "Life Cycles of Organizations and Programs."

1.   Do you recognize which life cycle your nonprofit organization is in? What are you seeing or hearing that leads you to make that conclusion? What is the next life cycle for your organization? What traits might you expect to see?

2.   What about each of its programs? What are you seeing or hearing that leads you to make that conclusion? What is the next life cycle for the program? What traits might you expect to see?

3.   What about your role in the organization? What are you seeing or hearing that leads you to make that conclusion? What is the next life cycle for your role? What traits might you expect to see?

You might even think about your professional career. What life cycle is it in? What are you seeing or hearing that leads you to make that conclusion? What is the next life cycle for your career? What traits might you expect to see?

Understanding General Planning Process

Whether you are planning your program's design, marketing or evaluation, you will benefit from a clear understanding of the process and terms used in most types of planning. You will need your knowledge and expertise about planning, particularly during strategic planning, market planning and operations/management planning for your programs.

Basic Planning Process and Terms

Remember the review of systems as explained earlier in this Field Guide? The planning process is the same as working one's way backwards through the system of an organization or program. The planner starts by identifying what goals are to be achieved, what processes are needed to achieve the goals, and then what resources are needed to conduct those processes.

There are various types of plans and various views about how those plans should be carried out. Planners typically use some or all of the following basic terms. It is not critical to grasp completely accurate definitions of each. Rather, it is more important for planners to have a basic sense for the difference between results (vision, goals and objectives) and the methods (values, strategies and tactics) to achieve the results.

1. **Vision**
    Some planners might start their planning process by clarifying the vision for their organization. The vision is depiction of the condition and activities of an organization and its groups of clients at some point in the future, for example, after the clients have benefited from the organization's programs. The vision often gives direction and inspiration to the organization and its program staff. The vision is often described in the form of a vision statement.

2. **Mission**
    Some planners might start their planning process by clarifying the purpose, or mission, of their organization. The mission answers the question, "The purpose of our organization is to _____." The mission is often described in the form of a mission statement.

3. **Values**
    Some planners might prefer to establish certain values that represent the overall priorities in the nature of how they want their organization to operate. For example, it may be important for the organization to operate with high priority on respect, teamwork and responsibility. The values are often described in the form of a values statement.

4. **Goals**
    Goals are specific accomplishments that must be accomplished in total, or in some combination, to achieve some larger, overall desired result, or vision. Ideally, goals are specified in terms that are SMART, an acronym for specific, measurable, achievable, relevant and timely. Goals can be in regard to impacts (outcomes) on clients or activities conducted by an organization or clients.

5. **Strategies**
    Strategies are the methods or processes required in total, or in some combination, to achieve the goals.

6. **Objectives**
   Objectives are specific accomplishments that must be accomplished in total, or in some combination, to implement the strategies.

7. **Tactics**
   Some planners, especially when working with very large plans, choose to specify a series of activities that must be accomplished in total, or in some combination, to achieve the objectives. Some planners might interchange use of the words "objectives" and "tactics," as well.

8. **Resources**
   Resources include the people, tools, supplies, facilities, materials, technologies, money, etc., required to implement the strategies and achieve the goals. Budgets depict the monies necessary to obtain and support the use of the resources.

9. **Responsibilities**
   These are listings of the specific individuals who are ultimately responsible to achieve the goals and/or objectives.

10. **Timelines**
    These are the times when the goals and/or objectives should be started, stopped and/or achieved.

Fundraisers often prefer the terms "goals," "methods" and "objectives" in grant proposals (written requests to funders). In this context, the "goal" is the overall accomplishment, or vision, to be accomplished by the program and the "methods" and "objectives" are the strategies and objectives used to achieve the goal.

Guidelines to Ensure Successful Planning and Implementation

A common failure in many kinds of planning is that the plans are never really implemented. Instead, planners place all of their focus on writing the plan document. Then, far too often, the plan just sits, collecting dust on a shelf. The following guidelines help you to ensure that your planning process – for any kind of planning – is carried out completely and that your plan is implemented completely, as well. The guidelines also help to ensure that any deviations from the plan are recognized and that plans are adjusted as necessary.

Be Sure Board of Directors Supports Planning

One of the major responsibilities of the Board is to establish the overall direction of the nonprofit and ensure that the nonprofit follows that direction. The Board carries out this responsibility primarily by overseeing the development and implementation of plans. This oversight includes official approval of the plans by the Board, as well.

Nature of Process Should Be Compatible to Planners

Some planners do not prefer the standard, general-to-specific, "linear" type of planning (for example, review and/or update the mission, vision, values, goals, strategies, objectives, responsibilities, timelines and budgeting). Instead, these planners might prefer more "organic," unfolding types of planning, for example, first focusing on values, reflecting on ideas about how those values could be "lived out," and then writing those ideas down on a semi-formal action plan.

Involve Right People in Planning Process

When planning, as much as possible, get input from the individuals who will be responsible for implementation of the plan, along with representatives from groups who will be affected by the plan. Of course, people also should be involved if they will be responsible to review and authorize the plan.

Be Sure Plan Is Realistic

Planning can be a very divergent and exciting experience. Do not succumb to over-emotionalism and fantasy. Especially regarding the vision, goals and strategies, always ask: "Can we really do this? How will we free up time and resources? By when? What resources do we really need? How will we get those resources? What if we cannot get them?"

Specify Goals and Objectives to Be "SMART"

As much as possible, strive to have SMART goals. As already mentioned, SMART is an acronym for:

1. **Specific**
   For example, it is difficult to know what someone should be doing if they are to pursue the goal to "work on a paper." It is easier to recognize "Write a paper."

2. **Measurable**
   It is difficult to know what the scope of "Writing a paper" really is. It is easier to appreciate that effort if the goal is "Write a 30-page paper."

3. **Achievable**
   It should be realistic to be able to achieve the goal in a preferred time frame. A person should not be assigned to write a 1,000-page paper overnight.

4. **Relevant**
   The goal should be closely related to the overall purpose of the plan. A person should not be assigned a goal of "cleaning the facilities" if their major role is to write a 100-page research paper over the next week.

5. **Timely**
   It is meaningful to commit to a realistic goal to "Write a 30-page paper in one week." However, that commitment is even more meaningful if the paper will get done just in time for inclusion in a major publication. In this situation, the one-week deadline is very important.

Build in Structures for Accountability of Goal Completion

Plans should specify who is responsible for achieving each result, including for each goal and objective. Dates should be set for completion of each result, as well. Be sure to have someone of authority "sign off" on the plan by putting their signature on the plan to indicate they agree with and support its contents. Ideally, those who are responsible to execute the plan should also sign off on the plan. Include responsibilities for completion of the plan in relevant policies, procedures, job descriptions, performance review processes, etc.

Have an Implementation Section in all plans. The section should at least specify what goals and objectives will be met, who is responsible to meet them and the deadline for meeting them.

Record Planning Information and Communicate Widely

New managers, in particular, often forget that others do not know what the managers know. Even if managers do communicate their plans verbally, chances are great that others will not completely hear or understand those plans. Also, as plans change, it is extremely difficult to remember who is supposed to be doing what and according to which version of the plan. Therefore, it is critical to write plans down and communicate them widely.

Key stakeholders may request copies of various types of plans, to understand the direction of the organization and ascertain the quality of its leadership and programs. Stakeholders include employees, management, Board members, funders, customers, clients, etc.

Note Deviations from Plan and Re-Plan Accordingly

Try not to see your plans as a set of restrictive rules that must be followed no matter what happens. That view can actually constrain the development and success of your plan. It also leaves many people feeling quite reluctant to engage in planning. A plan is an overall set of guidelines. It is okay to deviate from the plan. However, it is important to notice when deviations are needed or happening, the reason for them and how to adjust the plan as necessary.

Regularly Evaluate Planning Process and Plan

During the planning process, regularly collect feedback from participants. Do they agree with the planning process? If not, what do they dislike and how could it be done better? In large, ongoing planning processes (such as strategic planning, business planning and project planning), it is critical to collect this kind of feedback on a regular basis.

During regular status reviews of implementation of the plan, assess if the goals in the plan are being achieved or not. If not, were the goals realistic? Do responsible parties have the resources necessary to achieve the goals? Should the goals be changed? Should more priority be placed on achieving the goals? What needs to be done?

Finally, at the end of each planning activity, take 10 minutes to write down how the planning process could have been carried out more effectively. File your written notes and read them the next time you conduct a planning process.

Realize Process Is as Important as Plan

Far too often, primary emphasis is placed on completing the plan document. This is extremely unfortunate because the real treasure of planning is the planning process itself. During the process, planners learn a great deal from their ongoing analysis, reflection, discussion, debates and dialogue around issues and goals in their organization.

Perhaps there is no better example of misplaced priorities in planning than in business ethics. Far too often, people place most of their emphasis on writing the ethics documents, such as codes of ethics and codes of conduct. While these documents are very important, even more important are the discussions and debates to actually create the codes and then continually assess if the codes are being followed or not. The ongoing communications about the codes are what sensitize people to following the values and behaviors specified in the codes.

Acknowledge and Celebrate Achievement of Results

It is easy for planners to become tired and even cynical about the planning process. One of the reasons is that far too often, once the goals in the plan are achieved, they are quickly forgotten and replaced by new goals. It can seem like the planning process is just analyzing one problem after another, with no real end in sight. Yet when one really thinks about it, it is a major accomplishment to work with others to produce a plan, implement the plan and actually see some results. So acknowledge this – celebrate your accomplishment!

Guidelines for Successful Program Development and Evaluation

You might share the following guidelines with other planners involved in your program planning, such as a Board Planning Committee or Board Program Committee.

Plan Program Development and Evaluation as a Team

In the previous section about systems, you learned how important it is to consider all parts of a system and how they interact with each other. You also learned that it is important for all of the parts to continue to share feedback with each other. It follows then that key members of the Board, staff and major groups of clients should all be involved somehow in planning for program development or evaluation.

Ensure Program Is Closely Aligned with Organization's Mission

The goals of a program must be closely aligned with the nature of the organization's mission and goals. The organization's mission and goals are determined during the strategic planning process. Therefore, the program's planning process should be closely aligned with the organization's strategic planning process, as well. Typically, at a point right after strategic planning has identified overall goals, a team of planners can begin drafting frameworks for any new programs.

Involve Board Members

A major responsibility of Board members is to set the strategic direction for their nonprofit. Therefore, Board members should be involved in setting the overall direction for programs, as well. The Board might choose to focus its involvement in the form of a Planning Committee or a Programs Committee. Staff members must be strongly involved in the detailed action planning portion of strategic planning, including determination of how program services will actually be delivered to clients.

 For more information about Boards of Directors, see the annotated list of resources on page 243.

Involve Current and Potential Clients

One can embark on what seems to be a wonderful planning process for a new program to serve a specific group of clients. However, if key clients are not involved in the process to design the program, the organization might end up building a beautiful ladder – but entirely on the wrong roof. Programs are meant to serve the needs of clients. Therefore, clients should be involved as much as possible, including when specifying their needs and how their needs can be met effectively, what they are willing to pay for your program's services, etc. You might even have representatives from various client groups review the final draft of your plan.

Note that this involvement of clients is a critical aspect of the overall marketing process, specifically the aspect of marketing research.

Involve the Fundraiser

Effective fundraising for a program requires strong knowledge of the program, including its desired outcomes, how it intends to achieve those outcomes, and how it will verify whether those outcomes were achieved or not. Therefore, if you plan to raise funds for your program, whether you do it yourself or will use someone else, be sure that whoever is ultimately responsible for fundraising is also involved somehow in planning the program development or evaluation.

Do Concurrent Program Development and Evaluation Planning

A common mistake is to develop a program with little thought toward program evaluation, to operate the program for a year or so, and then set about to evaluate the program almost as an after-thought. When this sequence occurs, it can be quite difficult to effectively evaluate the program because the opportunities for gathering useful evaluation information have already been lost. Therefore, it is very important when first designing a program to give careful thought toward what kinds of evaluation information might be useful to collect during operation of the program. Then design the program to generate those kinds of information during ongoing operations.

Build in Key Indicators of Program Success

Know what it means for your program to be "successful." You will have to build in certain indicators of that meaning of success when designing your program. For example, consider a program to help participants achieve the outcome to "quit smoking." In that example, think about what you would deem as "success." Is success achieved when participants quit smoking within a certain timeframe? Is it when they have not smoked for some specific period of time? If so, what period? How will you know if participants have quit for that period or not? What indicators of success would need to be built in to the program for you to detect if the program was successful?

You might also establish certain goals and objectives for the program that, when attained, would mean success for the program. For example, your program might have a goal to develop and approve a complete Operations Manual that is fully approved by the Board Programs Committee. How will you detect if the Manual was completed or not?

Do not Worry about "Perfect" Plan

If the organization involves the right people in the planning process and everyone participates wholeheartedly, the organization will naturally develop its own "perfect" plan – the plan that completely suits the nature and needs of the organization and its programs. The organization remains the only real "expert" on its own planning process. Outside consultants and facilitators can be brought in, but each planning decision is ultimately up to the members of the organization. Plans are guidelines and should be updated as the organization develops and operates its programs.

Follow "20/80" Rule

An economist named Vilfredo Pareto once asserted that, in many important activities, the first 20 percent of effort generates the first 80 percent of important results. In program development and evaluation, start with the first critical 20 percent of effort that generates the first 80 percent of a good plan. The remaining 20 percent of a good plan often comes from actually implementing the plan itself. The guidelines in this Field Guide help you to quickly accomplish that first 20% of effort and then ensure that your plan is actually implemented, resulting in a 100%-effective plan for your program.

Have One Person Ultimately Responsible for the Plan

To be highly effective, planning for a program requires the participation of a team of people, including Board members, staff and, ideally, some current or potential clients. However, there should always be one person who is ultimately responsible for the development and/or implementation of the plan. This arrangement helps to make sure that the planning and implementation have clear accountability for completion.

Common Approaches to Program Planning

There are several common approaches to developing nonprofit programs. The particular approach used by a nonprofit depends on:

- **Nature and complexity of the organization's programs and services**
  For example, the process to develop a program that provides mental health services would probably be more complex than the process to develop a program that provides a food shelf to low-income families.

- **The resources and stability of the overall organization**
  For example, if the organization has been in operation for several years and its current programs have been using the same processes and procedures over those years, the organization probably has more accurate and reliable processes to design new or related programs. On the other hand, if the organization is relatively new, it very likely has limited expertise and resources to design its programs.

- **The extent of program development expertise in the organization**
  It is not surprising to find that many nonprofit leaders have very little, if any, formal training in developing programs. Many leaders have resorted simply to doing whatever seems most reasonable for their programs, while collecting as many resources as possible and hoping that they will be useful in the future somehow.

Following are descriptions of five common approaches to developing nonprofit programs. The nature of the approaches can overlap somewhat, especially between the approaches of "Build It and They Will Come" and "Seat-of-the-Pants" (both highly entrepreneurial approaches) and between "Nonprofit Business Planning" and "Nonprofit Business Development."

"Build It and They Will Come" Approach

In this approach, founders have a strong passion – even an obsession – about meeting what they perceive to be a major, unmet need in their communities. They base their belief almost entirely on their own perceptions, even though there is usually no verified evidence of a strong unmet need. In this approach, the founder:

1. Comes up with their own methods to meet the unmet need in the community.

2. Applies for funding, and often is turned down due to lack of research as to whether the need really exists or as to whether other nonprofits are already working to meet the need.

3. Advertises the program to the community, usually through word-of-mouth and sporadic flyers, brochures and direct mailings.

4. Can experience a great deal of frustration if people do not flock to the program.

5. Substantially increases the advertising throughout the community.

6. Either abandons the effort or, if the unmet need really does exist, persists and often accomplishes the seat-of-the-pants approach to program development.

Seat-of-the-Pants Approach

This approach is common to many new nonprofit organizations. In this approach, the nonprofit organization and its new program are so highly integrated that it is difficult to discern what resources go directly into providing services to clients versus those needed to run the entire organization. Therefore, the seat-of-the-pants approach to program development closely parallels the development of the organization itself, and might best be described as follows:

1. A person realizes a major, unmet need in the community. The person starts doing whatever they can to meet the need, mostly through their own efforts.

2. The person realizes that they cannot do it all and seeks help from others who start to chip in and help the person. Over time, all the people involved start to agree on who's going to do what to be more efficient. At this point in the program, all the participants usually are volunteers.

3. Over time, some or all of the people realize that they need more help, including money, to continue to meet the community need. To get funding, they form a nonprofit corporation by filing with the appropriate government agency. For example, in the USA, they would likely file Articles of Incorporation with the Secretary of State's office in their state. Filing for incorporation requires that the nonprofit has a Board of Directors. Next, they seek tax-exempt status from the appropriate government agency so they do not have to pay certain taxes. They might also choose to seek tax-deductible/charitable status. For example, in the USA, they would file with the Internal Revenue Service.

4. They continue to work to meet the major need in the community and to organize themselves, usually by recruiting a volunteer Chief Executive Officer and other staff members.

5. As mentioned earlier in this Field Guide, organizations go through life cycles. Nonprofit organizations and programs rarely get through the first life cycle until they have established the necessary processes and structures to sustain continued growth. Hopefully, in the seat-of-the-pants approach, members of the nonprofit realize that they need more planning to establish those processes and structures. If they do not achieve this realization, they can succumb to what is commonly called Founder's Syndrome, where the nonprofit is operated according to the personality of someone in the organization (usually the founder), rather than according to the mission of the organization.

6. At this point, whether the nonprofit achieves more organization of its resources or not, the nonprofit has developed a roughly organized program that is geared to meet the need in the community. The approach to program development was somewhat "seat-of-the-pants" in nature – people scraped the program together by doing whatever they had to and whenever they had to do it. The program just kind of came together.

While this seat-of-the-pants approach often works when first developing a nonprofit organization, it certainly is not always the best way to go forward or to add other programs.

Incremental Planning Approach

You can probably develop a new program without having to resort to the high-risk, seat-of-the-pants approach or even to a more comprehensive, in-depth process if:

- You know your client needs quite well (be careful about assuming that you do!),

- You plan to meet those needs by using program methods with which you are quite familiar, and

- The cost and risk of starting the new program are quite low.

If all of the above conditions are true, perhaps you can develop your new program with a straightforward project plan that specifies:

1.   Outcomes and/or goals for the new program to achieve

2.   Program methods to accomplish those goals

3.   Minor, or incremental, changes that must be made to current programs to implement the new program methods

4.   Who is responsible to implement the program methods and make the minor changes

5.   Timelines for achievement of the goals

6.   A budget that specifies the funds needed to obtain the resources to achieve the goals

Business Planning Approach

Usually a business plan includes descriptions of careful analyses of:

1.   A major unmet need among clients in the community

2.   Program method(s) to meet the need

3.   How the clients and program can engage in an effective, ongoing relationship with each other wherein the clients and program get sufficient value from the relationship

4.   How the program methods can be implemented and managed

5.   What the costs are to develop and implement the program methods

6.   How the program will be evaluated, including its process, goals and outcomes

There are a variety of views about the formats and content in business plans. Usually the overall business plan contains several other subordinate (or smaller) plans, including at least a marketing plan, management plan and financial plan.

You might have recognized that a business plan is essentially the same as a well-written fundraising proposal; thus, it might be said that the more you use a business-planning approach in your program development, the more probable that you will get funds from funders.

Particularly in the for-profit world, bankers and other investors often require a business plan because the plan includes a very careful look at all aspects of a project. Business planning is often conducted when:

- Expanding a current organization, product or service.

- Starting a new organization, product or service.

- Buying a current organization, product or service.

- Buying a new organization, product or service.

- Working to improve the management of a current organization, product or service.

You should consider developing a business plan for a nonprofit program, especially if any of the following conditions exist:

1.   The nature of the new program is new to your organization.

2.   You will need funding to develop and operate the program.

3.   You are not very familiar with the program's clients and their needs.

4.   You are not completely sure how to meet their needs.

 PART IV includes an example of the Table of Contents of a business plan on page 125.

Business Development Approach

"Nonprofits have to recognize that they are businesses, not just causes. There's a way to combine the very best of the not-for-profit, philanthropic world with the very best of the for-profit, enterprising world. This hybrid is the wave of the future for both profit and nonprofit companies."

-- from "Genius At Work," an interview with Bill Strickland,
CEO of Manchester Craftsmen's Guide and the Bidwell Training Center

A new trend in nonprofit program planning is nonprofit business development, which might take program planning to an even higher level of quality than business planning. Nonprofit business development includes the business planning process, so technically business development and business planning are not completely separate approaches to developing programs. However, in business development, there is usually more upfront, rigorous examination for opportunities to provide products and services among a variety of stakeholders to generate revenue that can be used to meet the mission of the organization. Business development often helps groups of clients and nonprofits to identify new needs that they did not even realize, whereas business planning often focuses on one already-known need. Thus, business development is quite market-driven, whereas business planning is usually program-driven.

Andy Horsnell, independent consultant, describes the main phases in the business development process as:

1.   Clarifying the current, overall situation of the nonprofit and its external environment, particularly to ensure a solid base from which to develop current or new programs.

2.   Inventorying the assets and capabilities of the nonprofit, particularly those that can contribute toward developing current or new programs.

3.   Brainstorming, screening and selecting a short list of opportunities in which to sell products or services, particularly those that might be used to deliver more of current programs to current clients, new programs to current clients, current programs to new clients, and new programs to new clients.

4.   Researching the short list for feasibility and selecting the most appropriate opportunities. For each opportunity, this includes careful consideration of likely sales and profitability, business models, payers and competitors, processes and materials required to develop each idea, and influence of laws and regulations.

5.   Strategizing and planning to pursue the selected opportunities, including developing a business plan for each opportunity.

6.   Implementing the plans and adjusting them to reality during implementation.

Approaches and Good Program Management

The business planning and business development approaches are usually much more comprehensive and in-depth than the "build it and they will come" and seat-of-the-pants approaches to program development. The business planning and business development approaches form the foundation for very good program management because the two approaches are likely to ensure:

- More accurate understanding of community needs

- Higher quality of service by focusing on what you do best

- More effective and efficient operations in your organization

- Increased financial resources, especially through increased mission-related earned income

- Better use of financial resources

- More freedom and choices of resources to meet community needs

- Improved coordination between members of the Board and staff

- Better relationships with clients and other external stakeholders

- Enhanced credibility with clients and funders

So, rather than thinking of business planning or business development as approaches to program development, you might benefit most from thinking of the two approaches as good program management.

Strategic Planning:
Direction for Programs and Staff

The primary purpose and goals of a nonprofit and its programs should be established during the strategic planning process. Therefore, no guide about nonprofit program development can be complete without at least a basic overview of the strategic planning process. This section of the guide provides information sufficient for you to develop a basic strategic plan, in case your organization does not have one yet.

It is not within the scope of this Field Guide to provide comprehensive guidelines and materials for you to customize and implement a complete, in-depth strategic planning process.

For more resources on strategic planning, see the annotated list on page 247.

What Is Strategic Planning?

Simply put, strategic planning is clarifying the purpose of an organization, where the organization wants to be in the future and how it is going to get there. Thus, strategic planning in a nonprofit organization means clarifying:

- The purpose, or mission, of the nonprofit organization.

- The desired status, or vision, for the nonprofit and its clients at some point in the future, usually in the next one to three years.

- How the nonprofit is going to achieve that status, including by analyzing the external and internal environments of the organization, establishing goals, implementing strategies to achieve the goals, and by operating according to certain overall priorities, or values.

- Action plans, including specifying who is going to be doing what and by when to implement the strategies.

- What resources are needed to implement the strategies and action plans, including budgeting for those resources, such as people, materials, equipment and facilities.

- How to make sure that the nonprofit is on track to get there, including by implementing, monitoring and adjusting plans.

Strategic planning can focus on one organization, numerous organizations involved in collaboration, or even on one or more programs in one or more organizations. Also, strategic planning can be carried out in any of a variety of approaches.

Perhaps one of the easiest ways to explain strategic planning is by using a simple analogy. The following table depicts a comparison between strategic planning for an organization to vacation planning for a family.

Strategic planning is like:	Arranging a trip we will take
Mission is like:	The reasons we are traveling, for example, relax, gain renewal, strengthen the family, educational experiences, etc.
Values are like:	Our priorities in how we carry out our trip, for example, have a good time, listen, talk, quiet places, opportunities to meet new people, etc.
Vision is like:	Where we want to end up and what we will be doing at our ultimate destination
External analysis is like:	Checking the weather, road conditions, etc.
Internal analysis is like:	Checking our available vacation time, condition of our car, who can drive, etc.
Goals are like:	Major stops along the way
Strategies are like:	Major routes we will take to the major stops
Action planning is like:	Identifying who will drive each route, check the map, make reservations, etc.
Budgeting is like:	Identifying how much money we will need to spend and tracking our expenses along the way
Implementing and adjusting plans is like:	Getting in the car and starting our vacation, then noticing that some roads are under construction and changing routes, etc.
Evaluation is like:	Hearing from family members about whether they enjoyed the vacation and what they learned

All Else Flows from Strategic Planning

Strategic planning has significant influence on many aspects of the nonprofit organization. That is why the process is so critical to the success of the nonprofit. For example, strategic planning influences:

- The identification of clients (primary and secondary) to be served by the nonprofit

- How the nonprofit serves the clients

- What resources are needed by the nonprofit, including people, time, materials, equipment, facilities and money

- How the resources are structured and aligned with each other, including Board, staff and programs

- Goals for the Board, Chief Executive officer and staff

- Organizational and program budgets

- Performance management, including of the organization, programs, Board and staff

Developing Your Basic Strategic Plan

There are numerous approaches to developing a strategic plan and numerous formats for a plan document, as well. The following guidelines and examples will help you to develop a basic, goals-based, strategic plan.

 For a complete set of worksheets to draft your strategic plan, go to http://www.managementhelp.org/np_progs/sp_mod/sp_frame.htm.

Draft Mission Statement

The mission statement should succinctly describe at least the purpose of your organization and whom it serves. There should be strong alignment between the mission and goals of your organization and the goals of your program. Therefore, you should give careful thought to the development of your mission statement.

Example:

> "To support individual and community development in our county by ensuring all adults between the ages of 18 and 65 achieve gainful employment in the community."

Draft Vision Statement

Your description should depict the overall benefits that your clients will achieve from participating in your program.

Example:

> "Every adult in our county is fulfilled by employment that contributes to his or her individual and community development."

Draft Values Statement

The values statement should describe the overall priorities, or principles, that guide how you want your nonprofit and program to operate.

Example:

> "We believe that:
>
> Employment provides opportunity for adults to develop community and themselves;
>
> Every person deserves opportunity for gainful employment;
>
> Gainful employment of all citizens is a responsibility of all citizens."

Conduct Basic External Analysis

An external analysis looks at societal, technological, political and economic trends affecting the organization, for example, trends in donations, recent or pending legislation, federal funds, demographic trends, rate of access to trained labor and competition. In your external analysis, do not forget to look at stakeholders' impressions of the organization, including funders', clients', community leaders', volunteers', etc.

For a comprehensive list about external environment considerations, see http://www.managementhelp.org/plan_dec/str_plan/drvnforc.htm.

Identify the most important five to eight opportunities for the organization. Next, identify the most important five to eight threats facing the organization. Planners refer to this activity as part of the SWOT analysis. SWOT is an acronym for strengths, weaknesses, opportunities and threats.

Conduct Basic Internal Analysis

An internal analysis looks at all of the major aspects of the nonprofit organization, for example quality of the Board of Directors, staff, market research, program design, advertising and promotions, financial management, fundraising and evaluations. Appendix C includes an organizational assessment that might be used to conduct the internal analysis. Identify the top five to eight strengths of the organization. Next, identify the top five to eight weaknesses of the organization. This information can be integrated into a SWOT analysis.

Identify Strategic Issues

Think about your SWOT information. What major issues does your nonprofit face? If your nonprofit is new, major issues might be, for example, the Chief Executive Officer is not being paid, the Board is not achieving a quorum in Board meetings or there is no money at all. To identify the most important issues, consider the following guidelines:

1.   Ask whether the issue is important or urgent. Often, issues seem quite important when they really are only urgent. For example, changing a flat tire is an urgent issue – but you would never put "changing a tire" in your strategic plan.

2.   Deal with issues that you can influence. Issues that are too narrow do not warrant planning and issues that are too broad will bog you down.

3.   Issues should be clearly articulated so someone from outside of the organization can read the description and understand the nature of the issues.

Identify Goals and Strategies

Think about goals needed to address each of the major issues. Goals should be written to be as specific as possible. Think about the strategies to achieve each goal.

Example:

> Goal #1: Establish half-time, paid CEO position by September 1, 2006.
>
> Strategy 1.1: Obtain funds to pay half-time CEO.
>
> Strategy 1.2: Establish and operate Board Search Committee.
>
> Strategy 1.3: Search Committee recommends CEO candidate.
>
> Strategy 1.4: Board selects new CEO.

Develop Action Plans

For example, for Strategy 1.1 above:

Actions for Strategy 1.1	Deadline	Responsibility
1.1.1. Recruit fundraiser/trainer.	1/1/06	Board Chair
1.1.2. Schedule Board training about fundraising.	1/1/06	Board Chair
1.1.3. Conduct training.	1/21/06	Board Chair (via Fundraiser)
1.1.4. Draft fundraising plan.	2/1/06	Chair of Fundraising Committee
1.1.5. Board approve plan.	2/8/06	Board Chair
1.1.6. Implement plan.	2/8/06	Board Chair
1.1.7. Obtain funds to pay half-time CEO.	6/1/06	Program Director

For more information about strategic planning, see the annotated list of resources on page 247.

PART II:

PROGRAM PLANNING

Chronology of Activities in Program Planning

You can see from a quick review of the contents in PART II a variety of major activities must be conducted when planning a program, including:

1.   Laying out the general framework (logic model) for the program.

2.   Conducting a market analysis.

3.   Identifying what must be done to build the program.

4.   Determining requirements for ongoing operations.

5.   Identifying all monies required to obtain and support use of expertise and materials in the program.

Each of these major activities requires various specific activities, as well.

Activities in Program Planning Are Highly Integrated and Cyclical

Each of the major activities is highly related and integrated with each other. For example, the marketing analysis will very likely result in modifications to the logic model that was designed before the marketing analysis was conducted. Attention to planning the program operations will likely result in updates to the results of the marketing analysis. Similarly, the financial analysis will result in changes to the marketing analysis, as well.

Good program management should include continual attention to the overall design of the program, its markets, management and financial operations. Good management is not carried out in a particular sequence. Rather, managers attend to a wide variety of tasks, each of which affects the nature of future tasks and how they are carried out. The cyclical nature of good management is also the nature of the activities required to develop a program plan.

Different Writers Might Use Different Terms and Sequences of Activities

This Field Guide explains the activities of marketing, first by explaining how to conduct a marketing analysis. Other writers might suggest that you first identify specific marketing goals and then update those goals based on the results of the subsequent marketing analysis. Some writers will use the term "publics" for "markets," and "target publics" for "target markets." Some writers will use the term "products" to refer to products and services. Whatever the terms used by various writers about marketing matters, all writers agree that marketing is critical to the success of program planning and effectiveness.

For Established Programs, You Can Start Anywhere

Experienced car mechanics know that, to keep a car running in good condition, you need to continue to give attention to all the major parts and processes in the car. They know that you can start anywhere to give attention to the car and the car will benefit as a result.

Similarly, to keep a program in good shape, you need to look at all the major parts and processes in the program. If you have an already established program, you can start with any of the guidelines in PART II and your program will benefit as a result.

Program Planning Becomes Easier as You Practice It

It may seem a little clunky the first time around, but as you practice the various activities in program planning, you will soon become much more familiar with them. You will find your own way of planning that best suits your nature and needs. However, be careful not to skip any of the activities in program planning without first giving careful thought as to why you are skipping the activities in the first place. Organizations sometimes become lax about marketing efforts and end up considering marketing to be only advertising and promotions – pushing services at clients. That situation often results in the organization getting stuck in its current life cycle, experiencing the same problems repeatedly.

Regarding the Amount of Time to Do Program Planning …

Good program planning is the same as good program management – the activities of program planning should be ongoing and they should become second nature to program managers. The reward of working this continuous process is that organization members, clients, Board and funders recognize a well-run program and respond accordingly by supporting the program, and purchasing or funding its services.

Program Planning Should Follow Strategic Planning

To be successful, a program must be closely aligned with the mission and goals of the organization. Otherwise, the program and the rest of the organization sometimes conflict with each other, which causes confusing messages to stakeholders, disagreements between organization members, and overall ineffective and inefficient use of organizational resources. Therefore, if you have not conducted strategic planning over the past year, do so before you start your program planning.

Importance of Strong Marketing Orientation

Good Marketing Is Good Management

Far too often, inexperienced nonprofit leaders develop a program to meet clients' needs without getting any feedback from the clients to verify what their needs really are. Then the leaders make a strenuous effort to "sell" the program to the clients. These leaders have built a beautiful ladder – but on the wrong roof! That lesson often comes from painful experience.

Experienced leaders have learned that it is not their opinion that matters most regarding whether their program is needed or not. The opinion that matters most is that of the clients that use the program. The best way to continually detect what clients want, and are willing to make an effort to get, is through continued use of good marketing techniques. Good marketing techniques include more than continual advertising and promotions to "push" a product or service at a client. Good techniques – and good program management – include, in part, the activities of marketing analysis, in addition to advertising and promotions.

Think about a positive experience you had when you visited a company to use its services. In many cases, the employees probably observed your reaction to the service and asked you for ideas about improving their service – those employees had a strong marketing orientation. A marketing orientation is an overall attitude of the people in the organization. In this section of the Field Guide, you will learn a great deal about marketing. Share this information with your employees. Help them to gain a strong marketing orientation, as well.

Critical Role of Market Research

It is extremely difficult to develop and sustain a highly effective program without conducting at least some basic market research. Some people have a strong aversion to the word "research" because they believe that the word implies a highly sophisticated set of techniques that only highly trained people can use. Some people also believe that, too often, research generates lots of useless data that is in lots of written reports that rarely are ever read, much less used in the real world. This is a major misunderstanding.

Odds are that if you have some impression of a strong, unmet need in your community and how that need could be addressed by a nonprofit program, you probably have already conducted at least some basic forms of market research. For example, you have listened (a research technique) to others complain about the unmet need. You have read (a research technique) about the unmet need. You have watched (a research technique) groups of people struggle when their needs were not met. So market research can be very useful – and it certainly is nothing to be afraid of doing.

Market research has a variety of purposes and a variety of data collection methods might be used for each purpose. The particular data collection method that you use during your market research depends very much on the particular information that you are seeking to understand. Appendix E includes a list of standard data collection methods along with guidelines about how to use them.

Uses for Market Research

The following paragraphs mention some of the primary uses for market research. Useful data collection methods are associated with most of the items in the following list.

1.   **Identify opportunities for programs to serve various groups of clients.**
     Verify and understand the unmet needs of a certain group (or market) of clients. What do
     they say that they want? What do they say that they need? Some useful data collection
     methods might be, for example, conducting focus groups, interviewing clients and funders,
     reading the newspaper and other key library publications, listening to what clients say and
     observing what they do. Later on, you might even develop a preliminary version of your
     program that you pilot, or test market, to verify if the program works or not.

2.   **Examine the size of the market – how many people have the unmet need.** Identify
     various subgroups, or market segments, in that overall market along with each of their
     unique features and preferences. Useful data collection methods might be, for example,
     reading about demographic and societal trends in publications at the library. You might
     even observe each group for a while to notice what they do, where they go and what they
     discuss. Consider interviewing some members of each group. Finally, consider conducting
     a focus group or two among each group.

3.   **Determine the best methods to meet the unmet needs of the target markets.** How can
     you develop those program methods? How can you ensure that you have the capacity to
     continue to meet the demand? Here's where focus groups can really come in handy.
     Conduct some focus groups, including asking them about their preferences, unmet needs and
     how those needs might be met. Run your ideas past them. At the same time, ask them what
     they would need to use your services and what they would pay for them.

4.   **Investigate the competition.**
     Examine their products, services, marketing techniques, pricing, location, etc. One of the
     best ways to understand your competitors is to use their services. Go to their location, look
     around and look at some of their literature. Notice their ads in newsletters and the
     newspaper. Look at their web sites.

5.   **Clarify your unique value proposition.**
     Your proposition describes why others should use your organization and not the
     competition's. A particularly useful data collection method in this area is the use of focus
     groups. Get some groups of potential clients together and tell them about your ideas. Tell
     them how your ideas are unique. Tell them how you would want your program to be seen
     (its positioning). Ask them what they think.

6.   **Conclude if the program is effectively meeting the needs of the clients.**
     One of the best ways to make this conclusion is to conduct an outcomes evaluation.
     Guidelines are in PART III of this Field Guide. An outcomes evaluation often includes the
     use of various data collection methods, usually several of them, for example, observing
     clients, interviewing them, administrating questionnaires with them, developing some case
     studies, and, ideally, conducting a program pilot.

7.   **Conclude if your advertising and promotions strategies are effective or not.**
     One of the best ways to make this conclusion is to conduct a process evaluation. Guidelines
     are in PART III. Similar to an outcomes evaluation, a process evaluation often includes use
     of several data collection methods, such as observing clients, interviewing them,
     administrating questionnaires with them, developing some case studies, and, ideally,
     conducting a program pilot.

Developing Program Framework

Information in this section will guide you to address all of the major considerations involved in designing an accurate, top-level layout (logic model) of your program. The logic model is quite useful to keep clear perspective about the program when conducting your marketing analysis, operations planning and program evaluation.

When designing a logic model, considerations include:

- What community need the program will be designed to address.

- What changes (outcomes) the program hopes to help its clients to achieve.

- What processes the program will use to help the clients achieve the outcomes.

- What resources (inputs) are needed to conduct the processes.

All of the above design considerations must be based firmly on clear understanding of the market for the program.

 As you develop your logic model, do not forget the guidelines from the section, "Guidelines for Successful Program Development and Evaluation," in PART I.

At this point, you should have conducted strategic planning, at least for the coming year. You will need to reference your strategic plan as you design your program.

Note that, if your organization is starting its first program, your logic model will likely resemble a depiction of the inputs, processes, outputs and outcomes of the entire organization itself.

Consider designing the framework for the program with a Board Programs Committee or task force.

Assessment of Community Needs and Interests

A needs assessment is a set of activities carried out to identify the needs among a particular group of people. For example, trainers often use needs assessments to carefully clarify the needs among a group of learners to be sure that the training is carefully designed to meet those needs.

A wise principle among marketers is that there's a major difference between what people need and what they want. Although people often buy what they want, rather than what they need, funders often invest in what people need – and programs are usually successful in the long run if they satisfy what people need, rather than what they want. Thus, when conducting basic market research, attempt to find out both what people need and what they say they want.

Some program staff, such as in arts programs, do not see themselves dealing with client "needs" as much as with client interests. Still, it is often more useful for program planners to translate the interests to be in terms of needs. For example, regarding an arts program, clients who are interested in the arts might have needs for more stimulation, diversification and emotional intelligence.

Often nonprofit program planners believe that they already have a clear understanding of the needs among their clients. Even so, it is still good practice to verify the accuracy and clarity of their understanding by conducting some basic needs assessments. Funders will look for evidence of needs assessments in fundraising proposals seeking funding to plan and/or develop programs. Funders will look for measurements and statistics among client groups, rather than opinions and beliefs among program staff. Therefore, it is wise for program planners to understand needs assessments and conduct the associated research activities in a highly practical fashion.

Appendix E includes guidelines to design and implement research plans that can be useful during needs assessments.

Some Research Methods to Use During Needs Assessments

Program staff can often get a good sense of the needs among various groups of clients by conducting the following standard activities. Notice how each of the activities references some form of market research, for example, observing, listening, interviewing, questioning and focus groups.

1. **Reference the strategic planning SWOT analysis in your marketing analysis**.
    For example, identify what threats might exist to the various client groups because of trends in government programs, economy, society and technology. You might stop by the library and ask the librarian for sources of information about these trends. Those threats might present opportunities for your programs.

    The SWOT analysis is explained in a previous section, "Developing Your Basic Strategic Plan," in PART I.

2. **Listen to your staff members**.
    They often have a good sense about the needs of various groups of clients. Be careful not to just count on these sources within your organization, though – make sure that your research includes sources outside of your organization, as well.

3. **Observe and listen to your clients**.
    Where do they seem to struggle? What are their interests? For example, are they having difficulty getting to your facility? What are their complaints? What do they ask for?

4. **Conduct at least basic client satisfaction surveys by using simple questionnaires**. These will help you to conclude if your current program(s) are really meeting client needs. On the questionnaire, ask what other needs they have that are not being met.

    Appendix E includes guidelines to develop questionnaires.

5. **Include a few questions in your newsletter**.
    Ask clients to call a phone number to report their unmet needs.

6.   **On a yearly basis, invite 10-12 clients to take part in a focus group.**

Appendix E includes guidelines to conduct focus groups.

7.   **Study the results of your program evaluations.**
Evaluations can be wonderful means to help clients to really think about their unmet needs.

PART III of this Field Guide includes comprehensive guidelines to plan and implement program evaluations for a variety of purposes.

8.   **Network among clients and other nonprofits with missions similar to yours.**
Interview some of them. Over time, you might begin to hear about the same unmet needs among clients and organizations.

9.   **Read the newspaper.**
Notice current problems in the community. Notice "hot topics" that people might be interested in.

10.   **Talk to Board members.**
If you have been selective in recruiting Board members to your organization, you probably have Board members who represent a good cross section of the types of clients that your organization serves or wants to serve. Board members often know a lot about the clients that an organization wants to serve. Some of them may even be past clients.

Now Identify Most Important Needs to Address

Once you have identified a variety of unmet needs among various groups of clients, it is time to identify the need(s) you want to address with your nonprofit program.

As you consider the following questions, complete the worksheet, "Assessment of Community Needs and Interests," in Appendix D.

1.   What were the community needs that you identified during your needs assessment?

2.   What is your ranking of the various community needs in terms of the needs you most prefer to meet with a program? Consider:
a) Each of the various needs and their relationship to your mission,
b) Your passion to meet the need,
c) Your organization's current capability to meet the need,
d) The number of people with that need and
e) Whether the nonprofit can get paid for meeting that need.

3.   What is the overall, top-ranked major community need that your program intends to meet? Think of your description in terms of their need, not yours.

4.   Is the need urgent or important? For example, it might be urgent to lose 10 pounds, but it is important to eat right and exercise. How did you come to that conclusion?

5.   Describe what you believe are the cause(s) of the need. How did it come about?

6.   What research have you conducted to verify the existence, and your understanding, of this overall, top-ranked need in your community?

Now write a brief description of the need.

Example:

> Forty percent of high school drop-outs from our city's high schools are not able to financially support themselves within five years of quitting school, and 25% of this group is resorting to crime in their neighborhoods within the same five-year period.

 Complete the worksheet, "Assessment of Community Needs and Interests," in Appendix D.

Vision for Program Participants

Try to clarify the vision that you desire for your clients. A clear vision helps program planners to begin to identify the program's desired results and how those results might be achieved. Think about the ultimate impact that you want your program to have on your clients to meet their identified need.

 Complete the worksheet, "Vision for Program Participants," in Appendix D as you address the following considerations.

1.   What would clients look like, or be doing, after they have benefited from participating in your program?

2.   Is the vision realistic?

3.   Is the vision directly related to meeting the needs of the clients?

4.   Is the vision closely related to your mission? Should your mission be changed?

Example:

> The crime rate among our city's high-school drop-outs has decreased by 75% over the past five years, and 75% of high-school drop-outs over the past five years have retained suitable employment for at least the past 12 months – in large part because of our training program to help drop-outs obtain a high school diploma.

Desired Outcomes for Program Participants

You read about outcomes in PART I of this Field Guide. Remember that outcomes are described in terms of changed knowledge, skills, attitudes, values, perspectives, etc., among participants as a result of participating in your program.

Overall Outcomes

Think about what outcomes that you would like your program to help participants to achieve for themselves. What outcomes do clients need to achieve to have their need met? To identify outcomes, consider phrases that include "enhanced …," "increased …," "more …," "new …," "altered …," etc.

If this is your first experience in choosing outcomes, odds are that you feel a little confused and unsure about identifying outcomes. Do not be concerned about picking the "perfect" outcomes or "doing it right the first time." Your goal for now is to pick reasonable outcomes. You will learn more about the process of choosing outcomes by actually developing and running the program for a while and also by evaluating the program over time.

If you feel stuck, it might be helpful to first ask yourself, "What activities should our program conduct to help the clients to meet their need?" Then complete the sentence, "We would do those activities so the clients _____." The wording in this blank is often in terms of outcomes, or changes in the clients' knowledge, skills, attitudes, etc.

Note that it can be quite a challenge to identify outcomes for some types of programs, including those that are preventative (such as health programs), developmental (such as educational) or "one-time" or anonymous (such as food shelves) in nature. In these cases, it is fair to give your best shot to outcomes planning and then learn more as you actually apply your outcomes evaluation plan. Also, seek help and ideas about outcomes from other nonprofits that provide services similar to yours. Programs that are remedial in nature (that are geared to address current and observable problems, such as teen delinquency) are often easiest to associate with outcomes.

Choose the outcomes that you want to examine, prioritize the outcomes and, if your time and resources are limited, pick the top two to four most important outcomes for your program for now.

 Do not forget the guidelines in the previous section, "Guidelines for Successful Program Development and Evaluation," in PART I. They remind you to work in teams and be sure to have other people review your ideas, including about outcomes for your program.

Examples:

Outcome #1 – Drop-outs from our city's high schools obtain high school diplomas or equivalent levels of certification.

Outcome #2 – After getting diplomas/certification, participants obtain at least half-time employment or enroll in an accredited program to further their education.

Short-Term, Intermediate and Long-Term Outcomes

For an extra level of accuracy and credibility, you might consider different levels of outcomes, including short-term, intermediate and long-term outcomes. You might also consider when each of those different levels might be attained. Think of short-term outcomes in terms of changes in knowledge and skills; intermediate outcomes in terms of changes in behaviors; and long-term outcomes in terms of changes in values, attitudes, status, condition, etc.

The different types of outcomes among participants in your program and when those outcomes might be achieved depend on the overall nature of your program. For example, a program with a desired outcome of "participants pass a driver's test" might expect different levels of changes in participants and at different times than a program with a more complex, desired outcome of "participants live independently."

Complete the worksheet, "Desired Outcomes for Program Participants," in Appendix D, as you address each of the following considerations.

1. Start by identifying the desired short-term outcomes for participants in your program. Imagine your client three to six months after having completed your program. What useful knowledge and skills would they have attained in regard to achieving the overall desired outcome from your program?

2. Identify the desired intermediate outcomes for participants in your program. Imagine your client 12 months after leaving the program. What behaviors would they have attained in regard to achieving the overall desired outcome from your program?

3. Identify the long-term outcomes for participants in your program. Imagine your client 24 months after leaving the program. What values, attitudes, status, etc., would they have attained from achieving the overall desired outcome from your program?

Program Methods to Help Participants Achieve Outcomes

Remember the logic model from PART I? The program methods and activities are the "processes" column in that logic model. Now think about what your program has to do to achieve the vision and outcomes. This section of your program development plan is sometimes quite substantial.

You probably do not need to go into extensive detail about the program methods now; for example, you do not need to think about how much of each kind of resource that you will need. Think in terms of trainings to be provided, presentations to be held, services to members, displays for clients, procedures for clients and resources for clients. In an upcoming section about program operations and management, you will need to think more about what resources you will need, who will manage them and how, and how much the resources will cost.

Useful market research activities to identify program methods might include the following:

- **Focus groups with clients who have the unmet needs**
  Ask them about how the needs came about. Ask them about how those needs might be met.

- **Interviews with leaders of nonprofits that serve similar groups of clients**
  Ask them about their reactions to your ideas. You might even ask them about why they have

not pursued a program like the one that you are planning – obviously, this question could backfire on you if they use your idea to start their own program.

- **Interviews with funders to get their reactions to your ideas for your program**
  This information could be quite useful if you approach those same funders later on to seek funding for your program.

- **Interviews with experts**
  For example, you might interview researchers who have researched the problem or community leaders who want to address the problem.

- **Questionnaires to current and potential clients**
  These can be used to get clients' impressions of the unmet need and how it might be met.

- **A pilot of your program**
  A pilot can be very effective at verifying the design of a program.

 Appendix E includes guidelines about how to conduct the various data collection methods.

To initially identify the program methods, you might think about:

1. What are other similar nonprofits doing to achieve their outcomes?

2. What have clients said that needs to be done to meet their needs?

3. What do your staff members say that needs to be done?

4. Any advice from experts in the field?

5. What are the conclusions from relevant studies or research efforts?

6. Any advice from funders?

Now think about:

1. Are the program methods realistic?

2. Are the program methods related to your mission? How? If not, should the mission be changed and, if so, how?

3. What research did you do to select the program methods?

4. What research do you still have to do?

 Complete the worksheet, "Methods to Help Participants Achieve Desired Outcomes," in Appendix D.

Outcomes Goals/Targets and Indicators toward Hitting Targets

Outcomes Goals / Targets

Now that you have some sense about how your program might help participants to achieve the desired outcomes, you can establish outcome goals, or targets, for your program. Outcome targets are usually the number and percent of participants that you want to achieve a particular outcome.

Organizations may need at least a year to really get a strong sense for what the program can actually accomplish toward helping a particular group of clients to achieve a particular extent of outcomes. Still, it can be quite useful to set initial outcome targets and use them as a "stake in the ground" from which to monitor the activities and results of your program. Certainly, the outcome targets will change over time as you learn more about your program. For now, make a reasonable estimate.

Examples:

> *Outcome Target* – 1,000 teens (5% of teens in the city) quit smoking for at least one month, within 12 months of graduating from your program.

> *Outcome Target* – Fifty percent (200) of the high school drop-outs from the our city's high schools over the past two years obtain a high school diploma within six months after graduating from your program.

Now do a brief reality check on each of the goals:

- Are all of the goals directly related to meeting the community's need?

- Do all of the goals together encompass most, if not all, of what you would like to accomplish as an overall impact on your clients?

- Can your organization really accomplish the goals now, or at some time in the future?

 Fill in the outcomes and associated outcomes targets in the worksheet, "Outcomes Goals/Targets and Indicators toward Hitting Targets," in Appendix D.

Outcomes Indicators

Outcome indicators are observable and measurable "milestones" toward achieving an outcome target. These are what you would see, hear, read, etc., that would indicate to you whether you are making any progress toward your outcome target or not. Indicators are usually described in terms of numbers and/or percents.

As you think about selecting your indicators, remember the guidelines in the previous section, "Guidelines for Successful Program Development and Evaluation," in PART I. Have other people review your ideas for the indicators.

For each outcome target, think about what observable measures, or indicators, will suggest that you are achieving that key outcome with your clients. This is often the most important and enlightening step when designing an outcomes evaluation. However, it is often the most challenging and even confusing step, too, because you are suddenly going from a rather intangible concept (for example, increased self-reliance) to specific activities (for example, supporting clients to get themselves to and from work, or to stay off drugs and alcohol). It helps to have a "devil's advocate" when identifying indicators – have someone who can question why you might assume that an outcome was reached because certain associated indicators were present.

Examples:

> *Outcome #1* – 400 participants (50%) quit smoking by the sixth month after completing the program.
>
> *Indicator #1* – Total of 200 (50% of our targeted participants) have not smoked for at least 30 days as of their last day of participation in the program.
>
> *Indicator #2* – Total of 300 (75% of our targeted participants) have not smoked within six months after their last day of participation in the program.

> *Outcome #2* – 200 drop-outs from our city's high schools obtain high school diplomas or equivalent levels of certification within six months of completing our program.
>
> *Indicator #1* – Total of 80 (40% of our targeted participants) obtain a high school diploma/certification within three months after finishing our program.
>
> *Indicator #2* – Total of 160 (80% of our targeted participants) obtain high school diploma/certification within four months after finishing our program.

Now do a brief reality check by answering the following questions:

1.   Does each indicator clearly suggest progress toward achieving the outcomes target?

2.   Do all indicators together strongly suggest attainment of the associated outcomes target?

Fill in the indicators in the worksheet, "Outcomes Goals/Targets and Indicators toward Hitting Targets," in Appendix D.

Outputs/Tangibles Produced by Program Methods

Outputs are the tangible results produced from the methods used in your program. Thinking about the outputs helps program planners to identify what resources are needed to use the methods. Outputs are useful sometimes as indicators of progress toward achieving the desired outcomes. Outputs are also useful sometimes as products that can be provided (even sold) to clients. It is likely that your program will produce a variety of outputs.

Consider the number of:

- Clients served

- Courses provided

- Courses completed by clients

- Books developed

- Books read by clients

- Reports generated

- Revenue earned

- Revenue raised by fundraising efforts

- Cars fixed by clients

- Clients who failed the program

Preliminary Program Logic Model

As you read in PART I, a logic model provides clear depiction of the program, including its inputs, processes (or methods), outputs and desired outcomes. Some nonprofit experts might call a logic model a depiction of a sequence, or chain, of events. Others might call it a depiction of "theory of action." At this point, you can begin to fill in your own logic model for your program. The following guidelines will help you to construct a logic model to be used for your program development or evaluation.

Regarding the following guidelines, do not worry about developing the "perfect" logic model. Just write down what you know now about the planned or current program. Then have others review the model for you to get their ideas, too.

What to Include and What Not to Include

1. When developing a logic model of one of your nonprofit programs, include only the major, recurring processes in the program, rather than one-time processes. For example, do not include the initial activities to build the program, such as "construct the building" or to "register with government authorities."

2.   Your logic model should include primarily the processes required to continue to deliver services to your clients. For example, "hold training sessions for clients" or "conduct certification assessments of clients."

3.   The size of the logic model should be such that readers can easily study the model without extensive reference and cross-comparisons between many pages. Ideally, the logic model is one or two pages long.

4.   The level of detail should be sufficient for you to grasp the major items that go into the program, what processes occur with those inputs, the various outputs produced by the program, and the overall benefits (or outcomes) that occur for clients who have participated in the program.

 Fill in as much as you can of the worksheet, "Preliminary Program Logic Model," in Appendix D.

Marketing Analysis

A marketing analysis ensures that you really understand your various markets and what they need, they all understand you and what you can provide them, and all of you are meeting each other's needs in a mutually satisfying fashion.

Consider conducting the marketing analysis with the Board Marketing Committee or task force. If this committee does not exist, strongly consider developing that committee within the Board.

At this point, you will benefit from having designed the top-level, conceptual logic model of your program.

 If you have not yet, you should attend to the guidelines in the previous section, "Developing Program Framework," in PART II.

The results of your marketing analysis will be used in many areas of program development and operations. Thus, you should complete the marketing analysis before you go on to planning program development and operations, assembling plans or planning evaluation of a new program.

Target Markets and Their Unique Features

You very likely want your program to meet the needs of all of your future clients. Can your program realistically do this? It is important that your program start out successfully, and that it be seen by others as having a good chance of succeeding. It is usually far better to start your program by serving certain groups of people very well, rather than to start your program by trying to be all things to all people. Therefore, it is important to think about what specific subgroups of the overall group of clients that you can realistically serve and then to target your services toward those subgroups, at least for now. In marketing terms, these subgroups are called your target markets. You need to be clear about the target markets to yourself, your staff and your funders.

Consider all of the people who might have the unmet need that you have identified. Are there distinguishing features in common that might comprise various subgroups of the overall group? Often, those unique features point to further opportunities for your program to meet the needs among the target markets.

For example, in a group of high-school drop-outs, are there groups of unwed mothers, groups with disabilities, or groups whose members are concentrated around specific geographic areas?

Examples:

> *Target Market #1* – Drop-outs over the past two years from our city's high schools. (Three schools are located 10-15 miles from your program, so those drop-outs might need transportation to get to your program.)
>
> *Target Market #2* – Drop-outs over the past two years from High School for Unwed Mothers. (That school's drop-outs are likely to need day-care to utilize your program.)

Start by thinking about subgroups that might have demographic features in common. Your librarian can probably recommend some useful resources to help you to examine your overall client group according to the following features, and others:

- Age

- Disabilities

- Economic status

- Education levels

- Family structures (single-family, single head-of-household, with children, etc.)

- Health problems

- Language

- Location

- Race or ethnicity

- Religious denominations

You might also identify subgroups by looking for common values, preferences or opinions among the overall group of clients. Again, your librarian might be helpful. Some examples are:

- Affiliation with your organization (for example, have already used your services)

- Political or social action groups

- Exercising

- Hobbies

- Interests, for example, modern art or performance art

Think about which subgroups, or target markets, are most appropriate for your program to serve. Consider:

- Your organization's ability to serve them

- Their ability to use your services

- Their ability to pay for your services

- The size of the target market.

 Record your thoughts about the target markets in the worksheet, "Target Markets, Their Features and Benefits They Perceive," in Appendix D.

Perceived Program Benefits to Each Target Market

Now, for each target market, carefully consider what might be most appealing about your program to them. This is an extremely important aspect of your marketing analysis!

Think hard about the common characteristics of each target market. Consider:

1.   What could be most useful to them about your program, considering their characteristics?

2.   How could you customize the program to be most useful to them? For example, you could offer a low-cost, reduced-service version of your program for clients with low incomes. You could offer satellite locations around the city for clients who have little access to transportation.

You really should use some market research methods to identify what each target market might like most about your program. Note that your choice of marketing research methods depends on how suitable the methods are to the skills of you and your client, what both of you can afford, and how much time you both have to use the resources.

    When you select your research methods, remember to reference guidelines in Appendix E.

If you used research methods to identify the preliminary program methods when you were developing your logic model, you can probably use some of those same research results now. If not, you might consider the following market research methods. You might also use the following research methods later on when addressing considerations in the sections, "Packaging," "Unique Value Proposition," "Naming and Branding" and "Pricing Analysis," in this overall section on "Marketing Analysis." Each of those sections is best addressed by understanding the target markets and their preferences.

1.   Conduct some focus groups among each target market. Further clarify your understanding of them by asking them about their needs and unmet needs. Tell them about your ideas for your program. Ask them what they think of them. If they like them, ask them why. If they do not like them, ask them why not. Ask if they have any other ideas for your program. At the same time, you can conduct some research for their ideas about packaging and pricing, two topics coming up later on in this marketing analysis.

2.   You could apply some quick questionnaires to get their reactions and ideas regarding your program benefits for their specific target market.

3.   Try schedule interviews with some members of each target market. Add the results of these interviews to what you found out during your focus groups and from looking at the results of the completed questionnaires.

    Fill in the perceived benefits in the worksheet, "Target Markets, Their Features and Benefits They Perceive," in Appendix D.

Packaging

Packaging is how you configure your products or services to be most cost-effective and convenient for each of your target markets. Packaging is intrinsically part of the product or service. It is how clients experience your products or services.

Packaging also includes how you group your products and services together. You might package services to include various levels or a series of services. For example, clients might want to start, and pay for, basic levels and then progress to more complex, and probably, more expensive levels. This is particularly true with products and services that pertain to training.

When packaging your products and services in your program, think about how you can make it as convenient as possible for each target market to experience and benefit from your program. For example, if you strive to provide childcare to second-shift workers, you probably do not want to offer your child care services from 6 am to 6 pm.

If you already conducted market research to identify various target markets and their needs, you can probably use much of this research to also identify how they could best experience your program and, thus, how to package your program for them. One of the best ways to identify the best form of packaging is to conduct a process evaluation of the program after it has been in operation for a period of time.

PART III includes guidelines to conduct this type of evaluation.

Fill in the worksheet, "Packaging Analysis," in Appendix D, as you consider the following for each of your target markets.

1. How will they access the service, for example, should clients come to your facility, you visit their offices, or can you provide services over the telephone or Internet?

2. What are their capabilities to understand the program and how to use it?

3. What are the options for scheduling?

4. What are the requirements for variability in service time or content, either between markets or between clients within a market?

5. Are there any likely difficulties in using your service?

6. Are there any challenges in language in using your service? Need translators?

7. Note that some regulations in various countries (for example, the American Disabilities Act in the USA) require accommodation to people with disabilities. However, does your service need to accommodate disabilities that are more specific?

Unique Value Proposition

Your unique value proposition is your description of how you want your program to be viewed by your clients and why your clients should use your program, rather than meeting their needs in some other fashion. It is one of the most important considerations in your marketing analysis. It completes the statements, "We are the program that ____" and "Clients come to us, rather than our competitors, because ____."

Your methods of market research might be similar to those used when determining target markets and the best forms of packaging (reference those previous sections). Think about what is important to each of your target markets. Consider how your program is attractive and unique in addition to the service that it offers; for example, consider the following for each of your target markets:

- Easier access to services?

- Good atmosphere?

- Great customer service?

- Great location?

- High quality?

- Low pricing?

- Others?

 Fill in the worksheet, "Unique Value Proposition Description," in Appendix D.

Naming and Branding

To effectively promote your program, you need to establish a strong reputation, or brand, for your program. Usually this is done by also establishing a strong brand for your overall organization. Your unique value proposition contributes to developing a strong brand. Now you should start thinking about a name for your program.

As with other aspects of the marketing analysis, the choice of the research methods you choose to name your program depends on your skill level, the resources that you have available, what you can afford and how much time you have. The research methods that you used previously to determine target markets and their preferences might also be useful when determining a name for your program. Be sure to get reactions to each of your considerations for a program name, especially from potential clients and from Board and staff.

Consider that:

1.   You need a name that conveys the nature of the service and, ideally, your unique value proposition.

2.   You need a name that makes sense locally, but will still be understood if the program extends elsewhere. The name you choose for your service will be around for a long time and can have substantial impact on how your services are perceived.

3.   You have to be sure that you are not using a name that is already trademarked or service marked. You might verify this by:

   a) Looking in the Yellow Pages of your local telephone directory.

   b) Calling the appropriate governmental office (for example, contact the Secretary of State's office in the USA or contact the appropriate provincial office in Canada) to see if similar names are registered.

   c) Looking in any on-line databases of registered and applied-for names (for example, see the web site of the federal Patents and Trademark Offices at http://www.uspto.gov/ in the USA)

4.   You should not have a name that closely resembles an already established name in your geographic area or service field because clients will confuse your services with those referred to by the other name. The organization with the other name may even choose to sue you.

5.   Should you use a different name for each target market?

Note that you can likely benefit a great deal from hiring a marketing consultant to help you design and build your marketing materials so they effectively convey the personality, or brand, of your program and the overall organization. The consultant can help you with selection and design of:

- Name

- Colors

- Logo (text and image)

- Business cards

- Labels

- Envelopes

- Web pages

 Collect your thoughts in the worksheet, "Program Name Analysis," in Appendix D.

Pricing Analysis

Nonprofits typically do not place the same high priority on setting prices that for-profits do. However, funders will not support a program indefinitely, so the nonprofit is always wise to explore what revenue can be generated from a service to offset its operating costs. Nonprofits that rely on federal funding would be wise to plan programs that recover costs through fees because, at the time of this publication, the federal government is substantially reducing its contributions to nonprofits.

Two major strategies for determining pricing are cost-based pricing and value-based pricing. Cost-based pricing involves identifying the total cost of producing and providing the service, determining the desired amount of profit and then setting a price to achieve that profit. Value-based pricing involves identifying what the client perceives as the value of the service and charging accordingly.

Several major factors influence the pricing for a service. Strategic goals greatly influence pricing. For example, if the nonprofit really wants to get into a new market quickly, it might charge lower than usual prices to engage more clients in the service. Later on, the nonprofit might consider changing pricing if the demand for its services is very high or low. Competitors' pricing also has a major influence. If competitors are charging much less, the nonprofit might do well to lower its prices. Similarly, if the competitor is charging more, the nonprofit might consider raising prices.

Market research methods that you might use to research the best price to charge for your program might include the following.

- Conduct some focus groups among each target market. What price can they afford based upon the benefits that they perceive in your program?

- You could apply some quick questionnaires to get clients' reactions and ideas regarding your program pricing.

- Researching your competitors' services and pricing will influence the pricing that you use for your programs (see the next section, "Know Your Competition").

Fill in the worksheet, "Pricing Analysis," in Appendix D as you consider the following questions.

1. Is your nonprofit recouping your costs (time, money, materials, etc.) to provide the service? (Note that you will learn more about your costs after you have completed this marketing analysis and the operations planning later on.)

2. Is it affordable to clients?

3. Would a sliding-fee scale be better?

4. What about volume discounts?

5. What is the competition charging?

6. What should the new fee(s) be, if any?

7. How do you know?

Note that some program planners believe that because they are operating in a nonprofit organization, the organization should consider providing its services free. This is a reasonable belief. However, many program planners have found that if the program is offered free, some people believe that the services are probably of equal value ("if they are free, they must not be worth much"). Also, many clients might too easily sign up for the free program. Because they have not paid anything, they often do not have strong commitment to attend the program and they end up being "no shows." Remember that your program can include a fee for services and if your clients cannot afford the services, you might help them to seek funding. For example, you can seek grants to help offset program costs so the program can offer deep discounts or even free services to some clients.

Know Your Competition

Nonprofits exist to serve their communities. One would think that in this spirit of service, all nonprofits should collaborate for "the common good." However, nonprofits do compete for the attention, participation and money of their clients – and in many cases, compete for the same funding from funders.

It is a big mistake to avoid this section of the program planning. Funders want to know where your program might fit into their overall "package" of services to their communities. To know this, they will need to know what other organizations might be providing programs similar to yours. If they see that you have made little, or no, effort to identify potential competitors, the credibility of your fundraising proposal will be hurt a great deal.

There are other advantages to identifying your competitors. If another organization is already providing a service similar to that provided by your program, it will be quite painful for you to find out later on that clients were not using your program because they could get services elsewhere.

Most of us are used to thinking of direct competitors – organizations that have services similar to ours and provided to the same target markets. However, there are also indirect competitors and they can have a strong adverse affect on your marketing plans. Indirect competitors are organizations that, while providing a somewhat different service than that of your program, can affect your target market in such as way that it might not have a need for your program's service. For example, if your program aims to help high-school drop-outs obtain a high-school diploma, an indirect competitor might be an agency that provides services to reduce the overall high-school drop-out rate. Or, if your program aims to help people pass their driver's test, an indirect competitor might be a city program to increase the use of city busses in your area.

Think about how you will know who your competitors are for each target market, including what they offer, what they charge, where they are located, etc. One of the best ways to understand your competitors is to use their services. Go to their location, look around and look at some literature. Notice their ads in newsletters and newspapers. Look at their web sites.

 Fill in the worksheet, "Competitor Analysis," in Appendix D as you consider the following questions for each of your target markets.

1.   Who are your competitors?

2.   What client needs are you competing to meet?

3.   What are the similarities and differences between their products/services and yours?

4.   What are the strengths and weaknesses of each of their products and services?

5.   How do their prices compare to yours?

6.   How are they doing overall?

7.   How do you plan to compete?

   a) Offer better quality services?

   b) Lower prices?

   c) More support?

   d) Easier access to services?

Note that you might update the description of your unique value proposition and your pricing plans based on what you have learned from researching your competitors.

What Current or Potential Collaborators Exist?

Successful collaboration brings two or more organizations together to work in synergy. Synergy exists when the collaboration achieves results greater than any of the participating organizations could have done by working alone. In working together, there is an economy of scale, or sharing of resources, that lowers costs and focuses more resources on serving clients.

An increasing number of funders are requiring evidence of collaboration, or at least willingness to collaborate, from nonprofits that apply for funding. Many nonprofit leaders naturally struggle with the notion of collaboration, of sharing resources and control with other organizations. Thus, collaboration can be viewed as quite frustrating by nonprofit leaders. This dilemma invites leaders to carefully consider whom it is that they really want to serve. If collaboration will better serve clients (and it often will), collaboration should be attempted.

One of the best ways to identify potential collaborators might be to contact funders in your area. In addition to finding out about other collaborators, the funders might be impressed that you are actually willing to collaborate to provide your program and, thus, be willing to provide funds to your program. Other ways to find potential collaborators include looking at various directories of nonprofits, for example those provided by the United Way of America or National Council of Nonprofit Associations in the USA. In Canada, the CharityVillage web site (http://www.charityvillage.com) has links to lists of nonprofits, as does United Way of Canada.

 Fill in the worksheet, "Collaborator Analysis," in Appendix D as you consider the following questions for each of your target markets.

1.   Who are potential collaborators with your nonprofit?

2.   What client needs might you collaborate to meet?

3.   What resources might they bring and what could you bring?

4.   What could you do next to cultivate collaboration with other agencies?

Applicable Laws and Regulations

It is critical to identify all laws and regulations that affect how you develop and provide your particular services. For example, nonprofits that provide social services or health services often must adhere to certain rules and regulations about public health, confidentiality and record keeping.

 Fill in the worksheet, "Laws and Regulations," in Appendix D, as you consider the following questions for each of your target markets.

1.   What kinds of taxes might you have to pay? In the USA, contact the Internal Revenue Service (IRS). In Canada, contact the Canada Customs and Revenue Agency.

2.   What kinds of insurance might you need? There are various kinds to consider, including property damage, general liability, product liability, disability, Workers Compensation, business interruption, health and medical, and automobile. Contact your local insurance agent.

3.   What licenses or permits might you need? For example, do you plan to sell products that require a permit to sell?

4.   What kinds of contracts might you need? For example, you might want to hire suppliers and vendors. You may want to use sales contracts.

5.   What kinds of regulations must you follow if you plan to hire employees? You will need to look into various labor laws.

6.   What kinds of inspections might you need? For example, if you sell food products or provide health services, you will likely need to be inspected. Also, if you plan to construct a building, you will probably need a building permit.

Contact local government agencies to determine these laws and regulations. Also, contact nonprofits that have services similar to yours.

Intellectual Property – Copyrights, Trademarks and Patents

You may want to legally protect the unique combination of ideas, innovations, processes and materials (the "intellectual property") that produce the products and services of your nonprofit. Communities usually expect nonprofits to operate in the spirit of complete support for the common good of the community. For some people, this expectation might include that the intellectual property of nonprofits should be owned by everyone in the community, as well. Thus, these people might believe that a nonprofit should not seek to legally own – and/or seek to be reimbursed for duplication of – its products and services. However, even if a nonprofit does not seek to be paid for duplication of its products and services by others, the nonprofit should seek to protect the integrity of its products and services. This includes that their names not be used for other similar products and services and/or that other, poorer quality products and services not be confused with the products and services of the nonprofit. Therefore, the nonprofit should carefully consider legal protection of its intellectual property. Copyright law protects original "works of authorship." Patent law protects new inventions and processes. Trademark laws protect words, names and symbols.

Summary Description of Programs and Service

At this point, you have thought – and hopefully learned – more about your program and its service. You have clarified the service's target markets, benefits to clients, competitors, collaborators, pricing and naming. Now you are ready to write a useful description of your program.

 Complete the worksheet, "Description of Service," in Appendix D, as you consider the following questions.

1. The name of your service

2. What the service provides

3. The specific target markets and the benefits of the program for each of them

4. The price(s) of your program

5. How clients can pay

6. Forms and formats (packaging) in which the program is provided

Remaining Marketing Analysis Tasks and Considerations

Now look through the various worksheets that you completed while conducting your marketing analysis. Most of the worksheets left space at the end for you to identify any remaining tasks yet to be done or considerations yet to be addressed to complete that worksheet in the marketing analysis.

Think about who should be responsible to do each task and address each consideration and by when.

 Complete the worksheet, "Summary of Remaining Marketing Analysis Tasks and Considerations," in Appendix D.

Marketing Goals

At this point, you have given careful thought as to which specific groups of potential clients (target markets) have which specific types of needs, and as to how your program can be designed to meet each of those needs.

In PART I you read that program goals are specified in terms of either program activities or program impacts (outcomes) on program participants. In a previous section about developing your logic model, you thought about your program's outcomes goals in terms of outcomes targets. Now you are ready to begin thinking about goals that your program can accomplish in its marketing activities with clients. Often, the marketing goals are considered part of the program activities goals, as well.

Like any other well-designed goals, your marketing goals should be designed to be SMART, including being specific, measurable, achievable, relevant and timely. Marketing goals are usually desired numbers of desired kinds of activities among desired groups of clients.

Examples:

> - Place 20 ads about your program in various newspapers and magazines over a 12-month period, starting January 1 of 2006.
>
> - Sell services to at least 250 clients over the 12-month period, starting January 1 of 2006.
>
> - Publish two articles about your program and its unique approach to services during the 12-month period, starting January 1 of 2006.

Think about the marketing goals that you want to establish for your program. Be sure that you design them to be SMART. Do not worry about establishing goals that are completely accurate and appropriate. Odds are that you will modify your goals somewhat, especially after you complete your program budget later on, in your program planning.

 Fill in the worksheet, "Marketing Goals," in Appendix D.

Planning Program Development

As mentioned previously in this Field Guide in the section, "Chronology of Activities in Program Planning," program planning activities:

- Are highly related and integrated with each other

- Are often conducted in a cyclical fashion

- Might be called by different terms and be done in somewhat different approaches

- For established programs, might be started anywhere in the planning process

- Become easier as you practice them

 As you conduct the activities in this section, do not forget the guidelines in the section, "Guidelines for Successful Program Development and Evaluation," in PART I.

Guidelines about Estimating Costs

Program planning requires you to estimate the costs of personnel and other resources needed to develop and provide your program, and then to organize those costs in the form of various budgets. You will need to estimate costs, usually for:

- Personnel (hired part-time and full-time staff, contracted professionals, and any activities to recruit and support volunteers)

- Supplies

- Tools

- Equipment

- Facilities

Estimating Costs of Personnel

Note that when estimating labor costs of personnel, you will need to consider the hourly wage cost (in the USA, personnel paid on an hourly basis are considered "non-exempt") and monthly cost of salaries (in the USA, salaried personnel are considered "exempt"). You also should consider the cost of providing "fringe" benefits, such as medical insurance and retirement contributions. There are some tools that you can use to estimate these costs. First, you should have some basic idea about benefits and compensation.

Benefits

Benefits are forms of value, other than payment, that are provided to employees in return for their contribution to the organization, that is, for doing their job. Some benefits, such as workers compensation in USA and Canada, are required by law for certain sized organizations. (Some people see worker's compensation as a worker's right, rather than a benefit.)

Prominent examples of benefits are insurance (medical, life, dental, disability, worker's compensation, etc.), vacation pay, holiday pay, and maternity leave, contribution to retirement (pension pay), profit sharing, stock options and bonuses. Some people would consider profit sharing, stock options and bonuses as forms of compensation.

You might think of benefits as being tangible or intangible. The benefits listed previously are tangible benefits. Intangible benefits are less direct, for example, appreciation from a boss, likelihood for promotion or a nice office. People sometimes talk of fringe benefits, usually referring to tangible benefits, but sometimes meaning both kinds of benefits.

You might also think of benefits as company-paid and employee-paid. While the company usually pays for most types of benefits (holiday pay, vacation pay, etc.), some benefits, such as medical insurance, are often paid, at least in part, by employees because of the high costs of medical insurance.

For the purposes of estimating personnel costs, you might consider the cost of fringe benefits to be about 40% of the cost of the wages or salaries (that percentage is reasonable in the USA at the time of publication of this Field Guide). Note that fringe benefits are usually higher for salaried personnel than for personnel who are paid wages.

Compensation

Compensation is payment to employees in return for their contribution to the organization – for doing their job. The most common forms of compensation are wages, salaries and tips.

Compensation is usually provided as base pay and/or variable pay. Base pay is based on the role in the organization and the market for the expertise required to conduct that role. Variable pay is based on the performance of the person in that role, for example, for how well that person achieved his or her goals for the year. Incentive plans – for example, bonus plans – are a form of variable pay. (Some people might consider bonuses as a benefit, rather than a form of compensation.)

Organizations usually associate compensation/pay ranges with job descriptions in the organization. The ranges include the minimum and the maximum amount of money that can be earned per year in that role.

Employers have to pay various payroll-related payments. For example, in the USA, payments pay workers compensation and FICA (social security). In Canada, employers pay workers compensation and employee health tax.

Employees have certain monies withheld from their payroll checks. For example, in the USA, employees have deductions taken from their paychecks for state and federal income taxes, FICA (social security) and optionally, employee contributions to the costs of certain benefits, such as supplementary life, medical insurance and retirement. In Canada, employees have deductions from their paychecks for various provincial and federal taxes, Canada Pension Plan, employment insurance and optionally, employee contributions to the costs of certain benefits, such as supplementary life and medical insurance.

Salaried and Hourly Job Roles

In various countries, job roles in organizations often have two primary classifications based on the approach to computing compensation. These classifications include "salaried" and "hourly" jobs. The compensation of salaried jobs is usually based on a bi-weekly or monthly fixed amount. The compensation of hourly jobs is usually based on an hourly rate. In the USA, salaried jobs are referred to as "exempt" jobs and hourly jobs are referred to as "non-exempt" jobs, meaning whether they are exempt or not exempt from certain requirements of the Taft-Hartley Act.

- Unskilled or entry-level jobs are usually referred to as hourly jobs (non-exempt in the USA). Hourly jobs also usually get paid over-time (at least, in the USA and Canada) – they get extra pay for hours worked over 40 hours a week or on certain days of the week or on holidays.

- Professional, management and other types of skilled jobs are usually referred to as salaried jobs (or exempt in the USA). Salaried positions often receive higher compensation rates and benefits than hourly jobs, although hourly jobs sometimes can make more money than salaried jobs overall simply by working more hours.

Each job must have the same pay range for anyone performing that job – one person cannot have a higher maximum pay than someone else doing that same job can.

Salary Surveys

To estimate costs for personnel, it is quite useful to reference salary surveys for exempt employees. There are a variety of on-line salary surveys for nonprofits. The following sites about USA salaries might be useful.

Wage and Benefit Survey 2000 Highlights at
http://www.tmcenter.org/quarterly/wandb_7.html.

How to Conduct a Salary Survey at
http://www.tgci.com/publications/97fall/howcond.htm

The Nonprofit Times salary survey at
http://www.nptimes.com/Feb01/sr1.html

In Canada, the Statistics Canada web site includes extensive information about salaries at
http://www.statcan.ca/start.html

Estimating Costs of Materials

When estimating the costs of materials, such as supplies, tools, equipment and facilities, you will save a lot of time and energy if you:

1. Identify the materials that you will need (the worksheets in this Field Guide will help you) as specifically as possible.

2. Get access to the World Wide Web. You can access a great deal of information, merely by conducting various searches for materials. For example, numerous suppliers have their catalogs on-line that list and itemize costs for the materials.

3.   Make an estimation that is within 10% of the average of the costs that you are seeing for an item. For example, if you are estimating the cost of a piece of equipment and find that it is listed at $5,000 in one catalog and $7,000 in another, the average of these two costs is $6,000, so make an estimate that is within 10% ($600) of this average.

4.   Do not forget to access any prior plans or reports that you might have in your organization regarding program development and operations. Often they include quite useful information about actual costs.

Starting Your Program

This section helps you to identify the tasks and resource needs (people, supplies, materials, tools, facilities, etc.) to conduct all of the one-time activities to first establish your program. Too often, these start-up activities are forgotten during planning even though they sometimes involve substantial costs.

The nature of the one-time activities depends very much on the particular product or service that you are providing. For example, a tangible product might require careful design to ensure ongoing reliability with low-cost parts that can easily be obtained and manufactured. Services, on the other hand, do not usually require substantial attention to tangible materials; rather, careful attention must be paid to human skills, such as listening, presenting, problem solving and guiding others.

If you have identified a suitable collaborator(s) during your market analysis, you may want to determine the nature of your collaboration before you undertake planning how your program will be developed. The collaboration may well save you a great deal of time and energy while developing your program. Also, attention from all collaborators to the program development process will help to ensure that they understand and have strong interest in the success of the program.

Consider completing this section with a Board Programs Committee.

Activities to Develop Program

Major types of activities required to first develop a service usually include:

1.   Research and design the top-level layout (logic model) of the program. This Field Guide includes guidelines to conduct this activity.

2.   Conduct a comprehensive marketing analysis, including research, analysis, writing and reviews. This Field Guide includes guidelines to conduct this activity.

3.   Procure and manage the resources required to first build the service. This activity might require financial planning, fundraising, purchasing, storage and managing inventory, administrating supplies, etc.

4.   Build (and sometimes test) the first version of the service. This activity might require developing a prototype of the service, creating marketing materials (logos, brochures, web sites, stationery, etc.), testing the prototype with various groups of clients, refining the design of the service, documenting how to provide the service and training others how to use the service. This task might also include working with various professionals to get protection of intellectual property (copyrights, patents and trademarks).

Major Considerations for Conducting Major Types of Activities

When planning development of your service, the major considerations are about the tasks, expertise and materials required to conduct the above-mentioned four types of activities. Consider:

1. What tasks must you complete to produce and manage resources and then build your service? What tasks must be completed to obtain the necessary resources and build the service? Where will you get the guidance to identify these tasks? What will it cost to get the guidance to do the tasks?

2. What expertise (people) do you need? For example, you will need people who can comprehend the guidelines about designing a logic model and conducting marketing analysis, adequately document considerations and conclusions, conduct reviews with key members of the organization and use sufficient authority to make key decisions in a timely fashion. You will also need people to do the tasks necessary to design and build the service. What will be the personnel/labor costs?

3. What materials (tools, supplies, equipment, facilities, etc.,) will you need? For example, it will be quite useful to have access to a reliable computer system and general office materials. What other materials might you need? What will it cost to fix them up, if necessary?

Fill in the worksheet, "Planning Program Development," in Appendix D.

Planning Program Operations

Once the program is developed, you will have a series of recurring activities and expenses associated with producing and/or delivering the product or service. These activities are often referred to as program operations. There are a series of supporting activities to consider as well as the activities associated with the direct production or delivery. This section will assist you in identifying all of these activities and the associated resources. You will sum up those activities and resources as well.

Advertising and Promotions

Consider completing this section with a Board Marketing Committee.

Advertising and promotions activities are aimed at continuing to bring a service to the attention of past, current and potential clients. Both of these activities are aimed at moving the potential clients along a continuum from awareness of your program to a desire to participate in it. Advertising and promotions are best carried out by implementing an overall advertising and promotions plan.

Successful advertising and promotions also depend largely on knowing:

- What target markets you want to reach.

- What features and benefits you want to convey to each of the target markets.

- What advertising methods and media you will use for each target market.

If you have already completed a marketing analysis, you have a good sense about whom you want to appeal to (your target markets). You probably also know what you want to convey to them about your program, including benefits to each target market (what is in it for them) and your unique value proposition (why they should buy from you and not your competitors).

Use some basic research methods to determine what media and activities are most likely to be noticed by your various target markets. For example, some groups listen to the radio a great deal, some might read neighborhood newspapers, and others read Web sites. For each target market, you need to address the following considerations.

Fill in the worksheet, "Advertising and Promotions," in Appendix D as you consider the following questions.

1.   What do they read? Where?

2.   What do they listen to? Where?

3.   Where do they go? When?

4.   What language(s) do they use?

5.   Whom do they trust?

Now think about the various advertising methods and tools that you can use to reach each target market, for example, brochures, flyers, radio or television. Appendix F includes overviews of many of the major tools and methods. You might use different advertising methods for each target market and you might use more than one for a target market. When selecting the best tools to use, think about:

1.   Cost of using the tool

2.   Time to develop and apply the tool

3.   Expertise to use the tool

4.   Who will use the tool

Consider tools, such as:

- Brochures

- Classifieds

- Direct mail

- Displays/signs

- Neighborhood newsletters

- Newsletters

- Posters

- Press releases

- Radio

- Special events

- Word of mouth

Sales

Some people struggle to think of "sales" as being relevant in a nonprofit environment. They might have an impression that sales is pushing a product or service onto someone who does not really want or need it. That is an unfortunate impression. Sales should be a partnership between the provider and the consumer, geared to explore the needs of the consumer and the features of the product, and assess if there's a suitable match or not. If there is a match, the salesperson should help the consumer to take advantage of the features, for example, to buy the product or service in a manner that is as value-added, cost-effective and convenient as possible. This partnership is needed in the nonprofit world as well as the for-profit world.

Sales can be a strong component of your advertising and promotions activities. In addition, the budget for advertising and promotions is often determined as a percentage of the revenue expected from sales. Therefore, we will look at sales at this point in the guide.

Sales involves most or many of the following activities, including:

- Cultivating prospective buyers (or leads) in a target market

- Conveying the features, advantages and benefits of a service to the lead

- Closing the sale (or coming to agreement on pricing and services)

Sales forecasts (or projections about sales in terms of money made, units sold, etc.) are often used as the basis for determining how much to budget for advertising and promotions and for public relations efforts. Sales forecasts are often made on the basis of market research about the market and industry.

Good sales techniques usually require strong skills in questioning and listening. The best sales techniques also include strong customer-service practices. Current customers are often the best sources of customers for new products and services. Probably the best approach to ensuring strong sales is to know the needs of clients – this starts with effective market research.

Consider getting the help of your Board Marketing Committee as you think about your sales planning. Consider how vigorous your sales efforts must be. Reference your marketing goals to see what you want to accomplish with your marketing. These goals, in turn, suggest how vigorous your advertising and promotions, including sales, efforts must be.

Fill in the worksheet, "Sales Planning," in Appendix D as you consider the following questions.

1.   What target markets will be approached?

2.   How will each be reached? Consider methods, such as the phone, fax, e-mail, face-to-face or postal mail.

3.   How will you generate sales contacts and potential customers (or leads) among each target group?

4.   What personnel and other resources will you need to support the sale? What will those resources cost?

Reference the advertising and promotions techniques in Appendix F.

Customer Service

Consider completing this section with a Board Marketing Committee.

The for-profit arena has seen dramatic improvements in customer service because customers have become more discerning in their selection of products and services. Organizations are realizing that the best source of customers for new products and services are current customers – especially if their needs are being met.

Fill in the worksheet, "Customer Service Planning," in Appendix D as you consider the following questions.

1.   What policies and procedures are needed to ensure strong customer service? Consider training for areas such as questioning, listening, handling difficult people, handling interpersonal conflicts and negotiating.

2.   How will you detect if customers are satisfied with the service from your program? What data collection methods will you use? (Reference Appendix E.) How do you know that those are the best collection methods to use?

3.   If customers are not satisfied, what will you do?

4.   What personnel and other resources will you need to employ the policies and procedures and to address customer's concerns? What will the personnel and other resources cost?

Delivery of Services

Consider completing this section with a Board Programs Committee.

When first planning a product or service, you need to ensure that the program will have a continual supply of the resources required to effectively deliver services for clients. If the program provides a product, you will need to think about how the product will continue to be manufactured. If the program provides a service, you will need to consider how the program will retain the necessary expertise and other resources to provide the service to clients.

Major types of ongoing activities required when providing an ongoing service usually include:

- Purchasing supplies and equipment that are used during the delivery of the service, including identifying the suppliers.

- Producing the service or product, including reproducing resources delivered to or used during direct delivery of services.

- Delivering the service to the client, including contact time with the client.

Activities in the following administrative and support areas should also be considered now:

- Fundraising

- Office administration (office supplies, property management, clerical support, etc.)

- Bookkeeping and accounting (information management)

- Financial analysis (report generation and analysis)

- Computer system administration

- Professional services (lawyers, bankers, accountants, etc.)

Major considerations when planning ongoing delivery of your service include the tasks, expertise and materials required to conduct the above-mentioned major types of activities. Consider:

1.   What tasks are required to conduct the activities? How will you obtain the guidance to do the tasks? What will it cost?

2.   What expertise (people) is required? How will you obtain that expertise? What will your personnel/labor costs be?

3.   What materials (tools, supplies, equipment, facilities, etc.,) will you need? How will you obtain them? What will they cost?

Complete the worksheet, "Delivery of Services," in Appendix D.

Personnel Management

Consider completing this section with a Board Personnel Committee.

Now that you have considered the full range of activities required to operate your program, you can consider the "big picture" regarding the people required to perform these activities. Collect all the tasks and expertise identified in the preceding subsections of this section. Look for tasks with similar or related expertise to determine what tasks will logically be combined. Look for tasks that can be assumed by existing staff. What tasks may need to be moved to a different role to allow for the additional responsibilities? These considerations of how to assign and organize staff will be addressed here.

Assignments

Now you are ready to think about what roles will be assigned to do what tasks and how much time that you will need from each role. You may want to consider the time required in terms of portions of a full-time equivalent or FTE. You will need to include the ongoing activities identified in the previous subsections.

You will need to consider at least the following roles:

- Program directors or managers

- Clerical support

- Board committees (these are usually volunteers)

- Volunteers

- Direct-delivery personnel

- Professionals (accountants, lawyers, fundraisers)

Fill in the worksheet, "Personnel Needs," in Appendix D.

Organization and Management

Now that you have identified the required human resource roles and amounts (in full-time equivalents or FTE's), think about how your staff will be organized and managed. Consider:

1.   Do you have the necessary expertise in-house now or will you have to hire additional help? What additional help might you have to hire?

2.   How will your staff be organized? What roles will report to what other roles? (Make sure that each person ultimately reports to one person.) Will your organization charts need to change?

3.   How will your staff be paid? Consider compensation (pay) and benefits.

4.   How will your staff be made clearly aware of their responsibilities? Will you need to update their job descriptions?

5.   How will you ensure that employees have sufficient resources to carry out their responsibilities?

6.   How will you ensure that each staff member has adequate supervision, including clear goals, and ongoing delegation and feedback?

7.   What personnel policies will be needed or need to be updated?

For more information about resources to organize and manage resources, see the annotated list on page 246.

Materials (Supplies, Tools, Equipment and Facilities)

Consider completing this section with a Board Programs Committee.

Now that you have reviewed the areas of activities and identified resources required for them, you can capture all the program operational materials needed. Think about what materials are needed to support program operations. How will you get them? What will be the cost? Will you have to fix them up? Use the worksheets you already completed in this section.

General Equipment and Supplies

Consider, for example:

1.   General office supplies (paper, pencils, pens, staples, etc.)

2.   Postage

3.   Tools

4.   Computers and peripherals (printers, scanners)

5.   Data communications equipment (modems, networking, broadband, etc.)

6.   Telephones (single-line, multi-line, cell, etc.)

7.   Copier (black and white, color, stapling, etc.)

8.   Fax

Major Facilities and Equipment

Think about what major facilities and equipment are needed to support program operations. How will you get them? What will be the cost? Will you have to fix them up? Consider, for example:

1.   Buildings (materials and physical layout)

2.   Furniture (materials and physical layout)

3.   Offices and layout

4.   Office bays and layout

5.   Conference rooms and/or training spaces and layout

6.   Utilities (electricity, water, sewer, heat, etc.)

7.   Telephone and data communications cabling

8.   Cleaning services

Complete the worksheet, "Materials (Supplies, Tools, Equipment and Facilities)," in Appendix D. You can also use the "Summary Program Budget" worksheet to capture the costs associated with these materials.

Planning Finances to Operate Program

If this is your first time developing the financial information for a program, you might have the impression that financial planning is best left to the experts and that you should not do the planning yourself. Do not be intimidated. You can do the first 20% of financial planning that generates the first 80% of the useful information. The rest of the planning information might come from actually implementing your program plan. If you have been completing the various worksheets associated with the marketing analysis and operations planning, you already have done most of the work required to develop budgets for your program.

 When planning the finances for your program, do not forget to follow the guidelines in the section, "Guidelines for Successful Program Development and Evaluation," in PART I.

Consider completing this section on planning finances with your Board Finance Committee, particularly with your Board treasurer. The treasurer often has expertise about financial matters.

Finally, remember that budgets are not rules and regulations that are "set in stone." Like other forms of plans, budgets are guidelines. They are meant to provide direction and be a common frame of reference for ongoing communications. If budgeted amounts are not completely accurate, they can be changed later on. The key is to recognize the need for change, identify what changes need to be made, and then communicate the changes widely among people who are interested in, or will be affected by, the changes.

Note that it is not within the scope of this Field Guide to provide comprehensive guidelines and materials about financial management. Information in this section will guide you to develop a program development budget and a program budget, which are the primary budgets associated with planning programs. Near the end of this section, sources of additional information are suggested for you to learn more about financial management. Sources are also provided about fundraising in case that information will be useful to you.

Key Financial Concepts

Basic Terms for Program Budgeting

You should have some basic understanding of the following key financial concepts before you start planning your budgets because they are the most basic and important terms for program budgeting. Review the following terms in Appendix A.

- Budget

- Expenses

- Revenue

- Direct costs

- Indirect costs (sometimes called "overhead" or "administrative costs")

Several Types of Budgets

There are several types of budgets used in nonprofit organizations, including:

- **Annual budget or operating budget**
  Depicts the expected expenses and revenue for the operations of the entire organization, usually for over a certain fiscal period. Ideally, the operating budget is determined during strategic planning.

- **Capital budget**
  Depicts the expenses associated with obtaining major pieces of equipment or facilities, such as buildings, automobiles, large computers or large pieces of furniture. Capital budgets are not always done by every nonprofit organization. They are usually done when an organization expects to purchase major pieces of equipment or facilities.

- **Cash budget**
  Depicts the current or planned status of the cash in the organization. This form of budget is especially useful when analyzing whether there is sufficient cash on hand to pay bills that must be paid now or in the near future.

- **Program budget**
  Depicts the expected expenses and revenue regarding operations of a program during a specific period of time, often based on the organization's fiscal period, development time for the program or other time period preferred by a funder. Guidelines in this section are in regard to developing your program budget.

  Some nonprofit personnel and experts also use the phrase "program budget" to refer to a "functional budget" or "program-based budget." The latter two labels refer to a particular form of budget that is used especially by large nonprofits and organizes expenses into three major categories: 1) program, or direct, expenses; 2) fundraising expenses, that is, expenses incurred during fundraising; and 3) administrative, or indirect, expenses. This functional budget format includes three columns of financial data. This Field Guide addresses what is sometimes called the "summary," "simple" or "basic" program budget in which the three types of expenses are combined. Thus, the basic budget has one column of financial data.

How to Develop Summary Program Budget

Note that if you have been operating your program for a year or more, than you very likely already have a good impression of the actual expenses and revenues associated with operating your program. In that case, be sure to reference past information about actual expenses and revenues when developing your program budget for upcoming periods.

Identifying Program Indirect Costs ("Overhead")

Before you begin to develop your program budget, you should give some thought as to how you will identify the indirect, or overhead, costs of your program. This is an important consideration because many funders want to be sure that their donations (usually in the form of grants) are focused as much as possible on the program's direct costs (costs of resources that are used completely to provide services to clients) rather than on indirect costs (costs to run the entire organization or multiple programs).

When identifying indirect costs, think about what resources are used to support more than one program, such as:

- Management and office staff that support more than one program, for example, the Chief Executive Officer and office administrative assistant

- Contracted help (independent contractors) whose services benefit more than one program, for example, a fundraiser and accountant

- Facilities (rental, utilities, insurance and maintenance)

- Office equipment (computers, copier, fax, telephones, etc.)

There has been a great deal of attention regarding how to identify indirect costs of a program. One common approach is to:

1.   Add up all of the indirect expenses of the organization – expenses for all items that are used by more than one program, including costs of the Chief Executive Officer's salary, facilities, office equipment, etc. Assume an example of a total of $100,000 of indirect expenses.

2.   Estimate the percentage of indirect costs that your program uses. You might consider primarily the percentage of the Chief Executive Officer's time on the program; otherwise, it could be quite difficult to conduct any form of practical estimation. Assume an example that the Chief Executive Officer spends 30% of his or her time on the program.

3.   Apply that percentage to the cost of the item for the overall organization. Assume that the cost of the Chief Executive Officer to the organization is $70,000 ($50,000 salary plus 40% fringe). Then compute 30% of $70,000, resulting in $21,000.

4.   Include the resulting cost as the item on the budget of the program. For example, report $21,000 on the program budget as the item, "Chief Executive Officer." You should mark that item, for example, with a "1,"that will point the reader to "Note 1" at the bottom of the budget. "Note 1" will point to commentary that explains how the Chief Executive Officer salary was computed for the program.

A general guideline is to try to keep a program's total overhead costs to about 15% of the program's overall costs. Use of this Field Guide depends on the nature of the program's services and the life cycle of the program.

However you choose to allocate the indirect costs of your program, be consistent and explain your approach by including commentary at the bottom of your program budget.

There is a sample summary program budget later on in this section.

Step One – Select Time Period for Budget

It is common to develop program budgets that depict activities over the nonprofit's fiscal period. The fiscal period is selected by the nonprofit to represent the official 12-month interval in which the nonprofit operations, including financial information, are reported and measured. You might also choose a period that is associated with the time expected to develop your program or a time period preferred by a funder.

Fill in the time period on your worksheet, "Summary Program Budget," in Appendix D.

Step Two – Identify Program Expenses

Although it is typical to start program budgeting by identifying expenses, some organizations might have established a policy not to have their program's expenses exceed their program's service revenue (revenue earned from services to clients, rather than from fundraising). This policy is certainly standard in the for-profit world when balancing a budget. However, it is common among nonprofits that program expenses exceed earned revenue (this is a called a deficit) and that the deficit is made up by revenue from fundraising when balancing a budget. If your nonprofit adopts the above budget-balancing policy (expenses not to exceed revenue), start your program budgeting first by identifying your program revenue, and afterwards, identifying your program's expenses. Otherwise, start your budgeting first by identifying your program's expenses.

 When identifying program expenses, regularly refer to the information that you recorded on the worksheets associated with the sections, "Planning Program Development" and "Planning Program Operations."

At this point, it might be helpful to review the guidelines in the previous section, "Guidelines about Estimating Costs."

1. Estimate the direct costs of the program, starting with personnel costs. Estimate:

   a) Costs for salaried personnel, for example, managerial or supervisory positions, including salaries and fringe benefits (plan 40% of salaries as fringe)

   b) Costs for hourly personnel, for example, secretarial support (plan 30% for fringe)

   c) Costs for any temporary employees

   d) Costs for contracted help (independent consultants), for example, accountants, lawyers and fundraisers.

   e) Costs associated with making those personnel productive, for example, training, membership dues, and travel. Include these costs under "Personnel."

   f) Other(s)?

 As you identify your direct costs of personnel, fill in the "personnel" section in the worksheet, "Summary Program Budget," in Appendix D.

2. Estimate direct costs regarding facilities. Consider program:

   a) Furniture (desks, chairs, file drawers, tables, wastebaskets, etc.)

   b) Other(s)?

As you identify your other facilities costs, fill in the "facilities" section in the worksheet, "Summary Program Budget," in Appendix D.

3.   Estimate other direct costs. Consider program:

a) Tools

b) Inventory (materials stored and/or sold to clients)

c) Marketing materials

d) Documentation, for example, texts, manuals, etc.

e) Office equipment (computers, copier, fax, telephones, etc.).

f) Other(s)?

As you identify your other direct costs, fill in the "other expenses" section in the worksheet, "Summary Program Budget," in Appendix D.

4.   Now estimate indirect, or "overhead," costs. Consider the program's percentage use of:

a) Personnel (management and staff) who support more than one program. Start with total cost of these personnel, including for salaried and hourly personnel, along with fringe (benefits and taxes) to pay for each type of compensation. Include in "personnel" section of worksheet.

b) Facilities (rental, utilities, insurance, maintenance, etc.)

c) Office equipment (computers, copier, fax, telephones, etc.)

d) Other(s)?

As you identify your indirect costs, fill in the "personnel," "facilities" or "other expenses" sections in the worksheet, "Summary Program Budget," in Appendix D.

Step Three – Identify Program Revenue

When identifying program income or revenue, regularly reference the information that you recorded on the worksheets about pricing, marketing goals and sales. It is often easier to estimate the fees from clients and dues from clients because you have already given careful thought to these items during marketing analysis and operations planning. Be conservative in your estimates; otherwise, undue optimism will likely put your program in a tight bind for money, once the program starts its operations. If yours is a new program, you will not have much information that is verified from experience. As a result, you will need to make some estimates to the best of your ability – this is entirely reasonable. Obviously, you will not likely have all the grants that you would like to receive either. Still, consider the grants that you are going to pursue and depict those on your budget.

To include revenue on your program budget, estimate:

 As you estimate your revenue, fill in the "revenue" section in the worksheet, "Summary Program Budget," in Appendix D.

- Fees from services to clients or dues from membership

- Grants from foundations

- Grants from corporations

- Grants from government

- Individual contributions

- Government contracts

- In-kind donations (donated services and materials)

- Investment income

Now you need to make a minor adjustment regarding any in-kind donations. In-kind donations must be recorded as both revenue and expense. For example, if you receive $25,000 of in-kind donations from a corporation in the form of $15,000 of furniture and $10,000 of computers, you must include $25,000 as revenue and $15,000 and $10,000 as two separate expenses, one for furniture and one for computers. Include budget commentary that explains the in-kind donations.

Step Four – Balance Your Budget

Balancing your budget means making sure that the total of your expected expenses at least equals the total of your expected revenues. Otherwise, your program will suddenly stop operating when your revenue is all spent. While you might expect more expenses than revenues, you certainly must make plans for how you will address the difference between the expenses and revenues, for example, by fundraising.

To balance your budget:

1. Add up your total revenues.

2. Add up your total expenses.

3. Subtract your total expenses from the total revenues.

4. If the result is a positive number (0 or larger) then you are not expecting a deficit.

5. If the number if less than 0, you are expecting a deficit.

6. If you expect a deficit, you must decide how you will address the deficit. Nonprofits can address expected deficits by:

- Reducing expenses until total expenses are at least equal to, or less than, total revenues; and/or

- Increasing revenues until total revenues are at least equal to, or greater than, total expenses. Expected revenues are usually increased by raising prices and/or increasing amounts expected from fundraising.

Update your worksheets and program plans based on the results of having balanced your budget. For example, you may need to increase your marketing goals along with associated sales, advertising and other promotions. These, in turn, might cause increased marketing expenses and/or somehow decrease your program operating costs.

Step Five – Associate Budget Commentary

You should explain anything about your budget that might be confusing to the reader, for example, how you computed your indirect costs or any unusually large or small amounts on the budget. Your explanations should be in the form of brief commentary included at the bottom of your budget.

Step Six – Obtain Review and Approval of Budget

As with other major plans in your organization, your Board of Directors should review the budget, including the major expenses and forms of revenue. Any changes that Board members might recommend should be carefully considered and made, if appropriate. Then Board members should officially approve the budget. Include mention of their approval in the official Board meeting minutes. (Minutes are the official written description of the major actions conducted during the Board meeting.)

Implementation of Budget

As with other plans in your organization, the budget should be carefully implemented, including with ongoing monitoring and changing, as necessary. Guidelines about implementing plans are in the section, "Implementing Plans," in PART IV.

Sample Summary Program Budget Format

Program Budget for Fiscal Year 2006 (January 1, 2006 to December 31, 2006)

Revenues:	
Earned Income:	$
Fees from services to clients	$
Dues from membership	$
Government contracts	$
Investment income	$
Total Earned Income:	$
Contributions:	$
Grants from foundations	$
Grants from corporations	$
Grants from government	$
Individual contributions	$
In-kind donations	$
Total Contributions:	$
Total Revenues:	$

(continued on next page)

Secretary	$
Training	$
Membership dues to professional associations	$
Total Personnel:	$
Facilities:[1]	$
Rent	$
Utilities	$
Cleaning and janitorial	$
Insurance	$
Maintenance	$
Total Facilities:	$
Other Expenses:	$
Office supplies	$
Manuals	$
Marketing materials	$
Tools	$
Total Other Expenses:	$
Total Expenses:	$

Note 1: These indirect costs were calculated by multiplying the program's percentage of use of the organization's resource by the total organizational cost for that item.

PART III:

PROGRAM EVALUATION

Understanding Program Evaluation

Program evaluation has become one of the most important aspects of good program management. It has become standard practice for funders to require program designers to include program evaluation descriptions in their proposals, especially with focus on outcomes evaluation. Unfortunately, many people still react to the notion of conducting program evaluations with fear or distaste. One of the overall goals of this section of the Field Guide is to dispel that myth that evaluation is something to be feared and, in fact, to show that evaluation is similar to the process by which adults learn.

This part of the Field Guide will be useful to you if you are:

- Evaluating a newly established program

- Evaluating a program that has been in operation for years

- Designing an evaluation plan to include in a proposal for funding a new program

Similar to the activities in program planning, program evaluation activities:

- Are highly related and integrated with each other

- Are often conducted in a cyclical fashion

- Might be called by different terms and be done in somewhat different approaches, depending on the writers and practitioners

- Become easier as you practice them

 As you conduct the activities in this section, remember the guidelines in the section, "Guidelines for Successful Program Development and Evaluation," in PART I.

Myths about Program Evaluation

Myth #1: Evaluation generates lots of boring data with useless conclusions.
In the past, program evaluation designs were often chosen largely on the basis of achieving complete scientific accuracy, reliability and validity. This approach often generated extensive data from which carefully chosen conclusions were drawn. Generalizations and recommendations were avoided. As a result, evaluation reports sometimes reiterated the obvious and left program administrators disappointed and skeptical about the value of evaluation in general. More recently, especially because of Michael Patton's development of utilization-focused evaluation (*Utilization-Focused Evaluation Methods* by Michael Quinn Patton, Sage Publications, 1986), evaluation has focused on utility, relevance and practicality at least as much as scientific accuracy, reliability and validity.

Myth #2: Evaluation is about proving the success or failure of a program.
This myth assumes that success is implementing the perfect program and never having to hear from employees, customers or clients again – the program will now run itself perfectly. This does not happen in real life. Program success is remaining open to continuing feedback and adjusting the program accordingly. Evaluation gives you this continuing feedback.

Myth #3: Evaluation is a highly unique and complex process that occurs at a certain time in a certain way, and usually includes the use of outside experts.
Many people believe they must completely understand terms such as validity and reliability. But they do not have to in order to conduct an effective program evaluation. They do have to consider what information they need to make current decisions about program issues or needs. They have to be willing to commit to understanding what is really going on. Note that many people already undertake some nature of program evaluation – they just do not do it in a formal fashion so they probably do not get the most out of their efforts or they make conclusions that are inaccurate (some evaluators would disagree that this is program evaluation if not done methodically). Consequently, they miss precious opportunities to make more of a difference for their customer and clients, or to get a bigger "bang for their buck."

What Is Program Evaluation?

First, we will consider "what is a nonprofit program?" Typically, nonprofit organizations identify several ongoing, overall approaches to work toward their mission. In nonprofits, each of these major approaches often becomes a program. Nonprofit programs are organized approaches to provide certain related, ongoing services to constituents, for example, clients, customers and patients. Programs must be evaluated to decide if they are indeed efficient and, especially, useful to constituents.

So, what is program evaluation? Program evaluation is systematically collecting information about a program or some aspect of a program to make necessary decisions about the program. Program evaluation can include any of a variety of at least 35 different types of evaluation, such as needs assessments, accreditation, cost/benefit analysis, effectiveness, efficiency, formative, summative, goal-based, process and outcomes. The type of evaluation you undertake to improve your programs depends on what you need to decide about the program. Do not worry about what type of evaluation you need or are doing – worry about what you need to know to make the program decisions that you want to make, and worry about how you can accurately collect and understand that information.

Reasons to Do Program Evaluation

1. **Understand and verify the impact of services on clients.**
    These "outcomes" evaluations are increasingly required by nonprofit funders as verification that the nonprofits are indeed helping their constituents. Too often, service providers (for-profit or nonprofit) rely on their own instincts and passions to conclude what their customers or clients really need and whether the products or services are providing what is needed. Over time, these organizations find themselves guessing what would be a good product or service, and using trial and error to decide how new products or services could be delivered.

2. **Improve delivery mechanisms to be more efficient and less costly.**
    Over time, product or service delivery often ends up to be an inefficient collection of activities that are less efficient and more costly than need be. Evaluations can identify program strengths and weaknesses to improve the program.

3. **Verify that you are doing what you think you are doing.**
    Typically, plans about how to deliver services end up changing substantially as those plans are put into place. Evaluations can verify if the program is really running as originally planned.

4.   **Facilitate better understanding of what their program is all about.**
     This includes understanding of the program's goals, how it meets its goals and how it will
     know if it has met its goals or not.

5.   **Produce data that can be used for advertising and promotions.**
     Various forms of promotions can be enriched by including testimonials from clients.
     Evaluations can produce those testimonials.

6.   **Produce valid comparisons between programs.**
     The comparisons might be used to decide which programs should be retained, for example,
     in the face of pending budget cuts.

7.   **Fully examine and describe programs to allow for duplication elsewhere.**
     If a program is successful, it's a precious source of learning for nonprofits around the world.
     The designs of the program should be shared as much as possible.

Basic Ingredients for Program Evaluation

You Need an Organization

This may seem too obvious to discuss, but before an organization embarks on evaluating a program,
it should have established means to conduct itself as an organization. For example, the Board should
be in fairly good working order, the organization should be resourced and organized to conduct
activities to work toward the mission of the organization, and there should be no current crisis that is
clearly more important than program evaluation.

You Need Program(s)

To effectively conduct program evaluation, you should first have programs. You need a good
impression of what your customers or clients actually need. You may have used a needs assessment
to determine these needs – itself an aspect of evaluation, but also usually the first step in good
program planning. Next, you need some clear program methods to meet the needs of clients. These
methods are usually in the form of programs.

You Need To Make Important Decisions about Program(s)

Program evaluation should not be done for the sake of conducting a program evaluation. Otherwise,
the evaluation would lack purpose and focus and would likely result in an expensive set of activities
producing a report that sits collecting dust on a shelf somewhere. Program evaluations are
conducted to make important management decisions about the program, for example, whether the
program should be discontinued, improved, duplicated or expanded.

 PART I explains more about nonprofit programs, including their basic
parts and how to design a conceptual overview (logic model) of a
program.

Major Considerations to Designing Your Program Evaluation

The more focused you are about what you want to examine by doing the evaluation, the more efficient you can be in your evaluation, the shorter the time it will take you and ultimately the less it will cost you (whether in your own time, the time of your employees and/or the time of a consultant). The purpose and focus of a program evaluation depend on the management questions that need to be answered about the program.

Consider the following key questions when designing your program evaluation.

1. **Who are the audiences for the evaluation information?**
   For example, is the information for Board members, management, staff, funders or clients? Each of these audiences might want specific decisions to be made about the program. Also, they might require that program evaluation information be organized and presented in a certain manner to really be useful to them.

2. **What is the management decision that must be made about the program?**
   Usually, management is faced with having to make major program decisions due to decreased funding, ongoing complaints, unmet needs among clients, the need to polish service delivery, etc. Examples of management decisions might be: How do we describe program evaluation plans in proposals to funders? How do we address problems and improve the program? How do we discern if the program is reaching its goals, or clarify and verify what benefits clients are realizing by participating in the program? Management might also want to replicate the program, shut it down, or verify if funding should be renewed.

3. **What evaluation questions must be answered to make the decision?**
   For example, if the program decision that you need to make is in regard to improving the program, you might have a range of evaluation questions to answer, such as: What are the strengths and weaknesses of the program? Is the program achieving its goals and if not, why not? What is the difference between clients who succeed in the program and those who do not?

4. **What kinds of information are needed to answer the evaluation questions**?
   For example, if you want to know if you need to improve the program or not, you might need information on staff and client complaints, costs of the program, the number of clients that passed or failed the program, the changes that clients report from having participated in the program, etc.

5. **From what sources should the information be collected?**
   Should it be collected from employees, clients, groups of clients and employees together, program documentation, etc.?

6. **How can that information be collected in a timely and cost-effective fashion?**
   Can it be collected by using questionnaires, interviews, examining documentation, observing customers or employees, conducting focus groups among clients or employees, etc.?

7. **How can that information be analyzed, interpreted and reported?**
    How the information is analyzed and interpreted depends on the focus of the evaluation questions and on the nature of the information, for example, whether it contains lots of numbers or comments. How the evaluation results are reported depends on the nature of the audience and the management decisions that must be made about the program.

8. **Who should do what evaluation activities and when?**
    Ideally, someone from outside the program does the information collection, analysis and reporting. That approach helps to ensure that the evaluation is carried out in a highly objective and low-bias manner. However, it is often unrealistic for small- to medium-sized nonprofits to afford an outside evaluator. Consequently, it is important to select personnel who can conduct the evaluation in a manner that is as objective as possible. As important, is to ensure that the program operations are designed so they automatically generate much of the information that will be useful in evaluating the program.

Common Types of Program Evaluations

This section explains four of the most common types of program evaluations, including the management decision each typically addresses and the evaluation questions to consider when conducting each type of evaluation. The types of program evaluation described in this section include implementation evaluation, process evaluation, goals-based evaluation and outcomes evaluation.

Note that programs might conduct one or more of the following types of evaluations, or an integration of one or more of the following types of evaluations. Of course, the nonprofit might conduct an evaluation that is not of any of the following four types. Again, the nature of the evaluation that is carried out by the nonprofit depends on the nature of the program management decisions faced by the nonprofit.

Implementation Evaluation – What Are We Doing?

The purpose of an implementation evaluation is to discern whether the program was actually implemented as intended, to find out what the program is actually doing. Patton (*Qualitative Evaluation and Research Methods,* 3rd edition, Newbury Park, CA: Sage, 2002) suggests that, if an organization has limited resources to conduct an evaluation, there are many occasions in which an implementation evaluation would be of greater value than other types of evaluation. It is not uncommon to set out to implement a particular program design only to find out later that program staff has (often necessarily) modified the process, sometimes substantially. It is often of no use to conduct a goals-based, process or outcomes evaluation if you do not know what process your program is really using to reach the goals or outcomes in the first place. Therefore, seriously consider conducting an implementation evaluation.

An implementation evaluation gathers as much descriptive information as possible about as many aspects of the program process as possible. This is especially useful during the development phase of a program.

Some Evaluation Questions to Consider

The following list of questions is by no means a standard and required set of evaluation questions that must be addressed whenever conducting an implementation evaluation. Rather this list provides examples of evaluation questions to help you get a clearer sense about the purpose of an implementation evaluation and the nature of evaluation questions that might be useful when designing an implementation evaluation.

1.   What are the advertising and promotions, and sales and service activities of the program? Who has been doing them and how?

2.   How do clients come into the program? What information is gathered and how is it managed? What procedures and forms are used by staff?

3.   How do clients begin to take part in the program? How are they trained? What do they do? What do staff members do?

4.   What do clients report as their experience in the program? How do they feel? What do they see?

5.   What tasks, expertise and materials are used to deliver the services to the clients? How are they used?

6.   What is the overall sequence of activities in the overall process to serve the clients?

7.   How do clients leave the program? What do they do? What do staff members do?

8.   What are the strengths and weaknesses of the program?

9.   How does the implemented program differ from the planned program? Are those differences important enough to change the implemented program or planned program?

10.   What can be learned from monitoring and evaluation to improve future planning activities and to improve future monitoring and evaluation efforts?

 To design your implementation evaluation, follow the guidelines in an upcoming section, "Planning Your Program Evaluation."

Process Evaluation – How Does the Program Work?

Process evaluations are geared to understand how a program produces the results that it does. The focus is on "how" the program process works, not on "what" activities are in the process, the latter of which is the focus of an implementation evaluation. Process evaluations focus on the dynamics of the processes and activities in the program and how they influence each other to produce the results from the program. These evaluations are useful if employees or customers report a large number of complaints about the program, or if there appear to be large inefficiencies in delivering program services. They are also useful for accurately portraying to outside parties how a program truly operates (for example, for replication elsewhere).

Some Evaluation Questions to Consider

The following list of questions is by no means a standard and required set of evaluation questions that must be addressed whenever conducting a process evaluation. Rather this list provides examples of evaluation questions to help you get a clearer sense about the purpose of a process evaluation and the nature of evaluation questions that might be useful when designing a process evaluation.

1.   On what basis do employees and/or the customers decide that the program is needed?

2.   What is the general process that customers or clients go through in the program?

3.   What do clients consider the strengths and weaknesses of the program?

4.   What do clients like or dislike about the program?

5.   What do staff members consider the strengths and weaknesses of the product or program?

6.   What do staff members like or dislike about the program?

7.   What did staff members do to improve the program?

8.   What do clients and staff members recommend for improving the program?

9.   What are the differences in the program experiences between clients who successfully complete the program and those who do not?

10.   What is the best process for the program to use to achieve the outcomes desired for participants in the program?

 To design your process evaluation, follow the guidelines in an upcoming section, "Planning Your Program Evaluation."

Goals-Based Evaluation – Are We Achieving Goals?

Often programs are established to meet one or more specific goals. These goals are often specified in the original program plans, hopefully in terms that are SMART, including specific, measurable, achievable, relevant and timely. Goals-based evaluations evaluate the extent to which programs are meeting predetermined goals.

Types of Goals

Organizational or program goals can be in terms of:

- Activities conducted by the program, for example, teaching children, monthly presentations or building a facility. These are often viewed as system processes or activities.

- Activities conducted by clients, for example, attendance to programs or completion of programs. These might be viewed as system outputs or outcomes, depending on desired outcomes of the program.

- Changes among clients as a result of participating in the program, for example, they quit smoking or graduate from high school. These are often viewed as outcomes.

Do not Just Focus Evaluation on Attainment of Goals

A key to making these evaluations useful is to not just focus on whether the program is achieving the pre-selected goals or not, but also on information that might enrich understanding of other aspects of the program. Singular focus on attainment of goals can substantially limit the learning from the evaluation and impose arbitrary expectations on the program when goals change.

Goals should be viewed as major accomplishments intended to provide direction for a program and evidence of the program's progress toward achieving that accomplishment. The goals were established at a specific point in time based on what program staff knew at that time. It would be arbitrary and unrealistic to expect those goals to always be in place. As conditions change and programs work to achieve their pre-selected goals, it is wise to accept modification of the program goals to ensure that they remain relevant and realistic. Patton (*Qualitative Evaluation and Research Methods,* 3rd edition, Newbury Park, CA: Sage, 2002) suggests it may be much more meaningful to get at what changes the program produced among clients (the outcomes), and then call those the program goals.

In addition to assessing the extent of progress toward achieving goals, goals-based evaluation can also be enlightening about:

- How the program goals were established.

- How the program worked toward the goals.

- Whether the current goals are realistic or not.

- How the goals can be changed if necessary.

- Whether any new goals should be added.

- How the program can be modified to pursue the new goals.

Some Evaluation Questions to Consider

The following list of questions is by no means a standard and required set of evaluation questions that must be addressed whenever conducting a goals-based evaluation. Rather the following list provides examples of evaluation questions to help you get a clearer sense about the purpose of a goals-based evaluation and the nature of evaluation questions that might be useful when designing a goals-based evaluation.

1. How were the program goals established? Was the process effective?

2. What is the status of the program's progress toward achieving the goals?

3. Will the goals be achieved according to the timelines specified in the program implementation or operations plan? If not, why?

4. Do personnel have adequate resources (money, equipment, facilities, training, etc.) to achieve the goals?

5. How should priorities be changed to put more focus on achieving the goals? (Depending on the context, this question might be viewed as a program management decision, more than an evaluation question.)

6. How should timelines be changed? Be careful about making these changes – know why efforts are behind schedule before timelines are changed.

7. How should goals be changed? Be careful about making these changes – know why efforts are not achieving the goals before changing the goals. Should any goals be added or removed? Why?

8. How should goals be established in the future?

 To design your goals-based evaluation, follow the guidelines in an upcoming section, "Planning Your Program Evaluation."

Outcomes Evaluation – What Are Impacts on Clients?

An outcomes evaluation helps to clarify and verify what changes your program is helping your clients to achieve. In past years, evaluation measures tended to focus on activities rather than on outcomes, for example, how much money was spent or the number of people served. These measures assess activities and not changes among clients.

Program evaluation with an outcomes focus is increasingly important for nonprofits and is increasingly being required by funders. There are decreasing funds for nonprofits, yet there are increasing community needs. Thus, there is more focus on whether nonprofit programs are really making a difference among clients. Outcomes evaluation focuses on whether programs are really making a difference for clients.

Some Evaluation Questions to Consider

Note that an outcomes evaluation is similar to a goals-based evaluation if the goals are in regard to specific changes among specific groups of clients (outcomes targets). Thus, the evaluation research questions in an outcomes evaluation can be similar to goals-based evaluation questions. As with goals-based evaluation, questions should not focus solely on whether the program achieved its desired outcomes or not. Outcomes evaluation cannot help program staff to conclude if the right outcomes for the program were chosen, or how the program should best choose outcomes in the future. Consequently, program staff should choose evaluation questions beyond the questions specific to originally-specified outcomes.

The following list of questions is by no means a standard and required set of evaluation questions that must be addressed whenever conducting an outcomes evaluation. Rather this list provides examples of evaluation questions to help you get a clearer sense about the purpose of an outcomes evaluation and the nature of evaluation questions that might be useful when designing an outcomes evaluation.

1. How were the program outcomes and targets established? Was the process effective?

2. What is the extent of the program's progress toward achieving the outcomes targets among clients? (Note that subsequent evaluation questions in this list depend on the answer to this question.)

3. Will the outcome targets be achieved according to the timelines specified in the program implementation or operations plan? If not, why?

4. Do personnel have adequate resources (money, equipment, facilities, training, etc.) to achieve the outcomes targets among clients?

5. How should priorities be changed to put more focus on achieving the outcomes targets?

6. How should the timelines to achievement of outcomes targets be changed? Be careful about making these changes – know why efforts are behind schedule before timelines are changed.

7.   How should the outcomes targets be changed? Be careful about making these changes –
       know why efforts are not achieving the targets before changing the targets. Should any
       outcomes targets be added or removed? Why?

8.   How should outcomes targets be established in the future?

To design your outcomes evaluation, follow the guidelines in the next
section, "Planning Your Program Evaluation."

Planning Your Program Evaluation

This section includes guidelines to help you design your own program evaluation plan. The effectiveness and efficiency of your program evaluation depends on the clarity of the focus of the program evaluation. Questions in this section will guide you to design a highly focused program evaluation. Guidelines in this section are in accordance with those in a previous section, "Major Considerations to Designing Your Program Evaluation."

When planning your program evaluation, do not forget to follow the "Guidelines to Successful Program Development and Evaluation" in PART I.

Work with a team. Do not shoot for the "perfect" evaluation plan. Make at least the first 20% of effort needed to generate the first 80% of a good evaluation plan.

Note that the learnings from conducting a program evaluation can be used to 1) update several aspects of your program materials, including descriptions of the program processes/methods and outcomes in the design of the logic model, and 2) refine selection of the marketing goals or program activities goals.

Consider completing this section with the Board Planning Committee, Board Programs Committee or a Board Evaluation Committee, which ever of these committees focuses on program evaluation.

Should You Hire a Program Evaluator?

At the time of the writing of this Field Guide, there is increasing pressure on nonprofits to provide program evaluation plans in proposals to funders and to implement those evaluation plans during the operations of their programs. While the increasing pressure exists, there is also a quite limited supply of experienced, accessible program evaluators. Many of them work on large programs, such as those developed and provided by government agencies. Many small- to medium-sized nonprofits do not have the money to hire a program evaluator. Consequently, they are faced with designing and implementing a program evaluation plan by themselves.

Nonprofits can do much, if not all, of a program evaluation design and implementation themselves. They need commitment, leadership and patience. Guidelines about evaluation in this Field Guide are intended to help nonprofits design and implement program evaluation plans, whether they do the effort themselves or get an outside evaluator.

The hiring of an evaluator should be done in an approach quite similar to hiring any other expertise, including full-time staff. Write down what you require of the evaluator. Even consider drafting a job description. Compose a Request for Proposal from which several evaluators submit proposals to you, including how they would implement your program evaluation plans according to your requirements and what they would charge you as a fee.

Some nonprofits might secure a small grant to hire an evaluator. Costs of an evaluator vary, depending on the size and complexity of the program to be evaluated and on the nonprofit's expertise to help conduct the program evaluation. Sources of evaluators in the USA might be found by contacting the American Evaluation Association or by referencing the section on "Consultants" in your Yellow Pages. Sources in Canada might be found by contacting the United Way of Canada.

If you need to develop an evaluation plan based on a requirement from a funder to which you plan to submit a proposal, contact the funder to solicit ideas where to find an evaluator. Many funders are reluctant to expressly recommend particular consultants; however, they might have ideas on where you can find an evaluator if you are committed to having an outside evaluator work with you.

Who Is the Audience for Your Program Evaluation?

Whoever first asked for your program evaluation is probably a primary audience for your evaluation report. For example, is it potential funders? The funder who granted you the money to develop the program? Board members who wanted to know why you want approval to add or delete a program? Staff or clients who complain about the program? Program planners who want to know if the program plans are accurate or not?

Funders might be interested in a range of information. For new programs, funders may want to know what processes were actually used in the program, what results (including outcomes) were actually achieved, and what was learned from implementing and operating the program. Ideally, funders specify their program evaluation requirements in their grant guidelines. Evaluation reports to funders should focus primarily on what funders indicated that they wanted to know.

Board members, senior management and staff might want to know the same information as desired by funders. They are likely to also want to understand strengths and weaknesses of the marketing activities, whether the program was sufficiently resourced, how to polish the evaluation activities, whether the program achieved its goals or not, and ultimately, how to improve the overall program. Evaluation reports to Board, management and staff might include more detail than reports to funders and other outside stakeholders.

 In the worksheet, "Planning Your Program Evaluation," in Appendix D, complete the sections, "Name of program to be evaluated" and "Audience(s) of evaluation."

What Management Decisions Do You Need to Make?

Many managers want to know as much as possible about all aspects of a program. It is rarely feasible – and often, extraneous – to learn everything about a program. Learning everything would likely require vast resources. Most small- to medium-sized nonprofits do not have those vast resources to allocate to program evaluation activities.

Often, the more focused your program evaluation design, the more useful the evaluation results – and the more effective your use of resources to conduct the program evaluation. One of the best places to start to focus your evaluation is to identify what management decisions are most important to make about your program.

Management decisions are in regard to some overall potential change to the program. For example, keep it or shut it down? Put more money into it or cut back funding? Keep the current service delivery method or change it? Duplicate the program elsewhere or run it on its own for another year? Integrate it with another program or run it free-standing for another year?

To help you identify the management decision that you need to make (and you are probably faced with at least one, considering that you are interested in program evaluation at this point), think about who first asked for the evaluation. Why do they want the evaluation? The answer to this question usually points to a management decision that they want to make. For example, funders might want to decide whether to reinvest in the program or not, Board members might want to decide to keep the program or not, or program planners might want to decide how to improve the program.

Think about any ongoing questions that have been bothering you about your program. Then ask yourself, "What would you do if you had an answer to those questions?" Your answer to that question is usually about a management decision you would make. For example, if you have been concerned that your program might not be making any difference for your program participants, what would you do if you knew that the program was not making a difference? You would be faced with various management decisions. For example, should you change the program processes or stop the program?

What do you want to be able to decide as a result of the evaluation? For example:

1.   Do you want to verify that we are doing what we think we are doing (could suggest implementation evaluation)? (This type of evaluation is strongly recommended for new programs.)

2.   Do you want to understand, verify or increase impact of products or services on customers/clients (could suggest outcomes evaluation)?

3.   Do you want to improve delivery mechanisms to be more efficient and less costly (could suggest process evaluation)?

4.   Do you want to clarify program goals, processes and outcomes for management planning (could suggest goals, process and outcomes evaluation)?

5.   Do you want to generate information for public relations campaign (could suggest outcomes evaluation and goals evaluation, if public relations plan and goals had been established)?

6.   Do you want to conduct program comparisons, for example, to decide which program should be retained (could suggest process and outcomes evaluations)?

7.   Do you want to fully examine and describe effective programs for duplication elsewhere (suggests process and outcomes evaluations)?

8.   Other decisions that you face regarding your program?

You might want to rank which decisions are most important to make. That ranking will give even more focus to your evaluation, thereby, ensuring that the evaluation results are useful to you and that you make the most of your resources that you apply to the program evaluation.

 In the worksheet, "Planning Your Program Evaluation," in Appendix D, complete the sections, "Purpose(s) of the evaluation" and "Likely type(s) of evaluation."

What Evaluation Questions Should You Answer?

Your program evaluation should be focused on more than the general notion of addressing a management decision. The evaluation gains much more focus by associating specific questions that must be addressed. The questions should be identified such that, when they are answered in total, they provide sufficient information for management to make necessary decisions about the program.

Patton (*Qualitative Evaluation and Research Methods*, 2nd edition, Newbury Park, CA: Sage, 1990, pp. 116) notes that, "There is no rule of thumb that tells a researcher precisely how to focus a study. The extent to which a research question is broad or narrow depends on purpose, the resources available, the time available, and the interests of those involved. In brief, these are not choices between good and bad, but choices among alternatives, all of which have merit." Patton mentions that people may be inclined to include a large number of evaluation questions, wanting to know as much as possible about all aspects of the program. It is more important to select a list of questions that are *essential and necessary*.

Management decisions about programs are often posed in the form of questions, for example, "Should we continue or discontinue the program?" While management decisions are often in the form of questions, they are not usually in the nature of useful evaluation questions. Useful evaluation questions are usually about some particular aspect of the program itself, rather than about a major change being considered about the program. At this point, if you have not yet done so, you would gain better understanding about the nature of evaluation questions by reviewing the nature of the evaluation questions suggested in a previous section, "Common Types of Program Evaluations."

To help you identify what evaluation questions are essential and necessary, pay careful attention to the most important management decisions that you need to make. Then consider the evaluation questions that are suggested for consideration in the description of each of the major types of evaluation described in the previous section, "Common Types of Program Evaluation."

If Evaluation Includes Question "What Is Progress toward Achieving Outcomes?"

Planning around this evaluation question requires a slightly different set of considerations than for other evaluation questions. This question requires that you identify the program's desired outcomes and associated outcomes targets, if you have not yet done so. PART II provides guidelines to complete a logic model, including guidelines to identify desired outcomes for clients participating in the program and outcomes targets toward which the program should aim.

 In the worksheet, "Planning Your Program Evaluation," in Appendix D, find the sheet titled, "Outcome Measurement Framework." Write in each outcome and the associated outcome targets. Note that you will need to make a copy of that worksheet page for each outcome.

For Other Evaluation Questions

 In the worksheet, "Planning Your Program Evaluation," in Appendix D, find the sheet titled "Evaluation Questions and Data Collection." Fill in each evaluation question. Note that you will need to make a copy of that worksheet page for each evaluation question.

What Information Is Needed to Answer Evaluation Questions?

Now carefully consider what information is needed to answer *each* of your evaluation questions. The identification of information to answer questions is often a highly intuitive exercise.

To help you identify what information is needed, ask yourself, "What are you seeing or hearing that leads you to be concerned or interested in a particular aspect of the program?" For example, if you are wondering about whether to continue a program or not, what have you been seeing or hearing that causes you that concern? The answer to that question often points to useful information that you need to learn more about and that likely should be associated with a key evaluation question. If there is not an evaluation question for that information, maybe you need to include one in your evaluation design.

Another approach might be to imagine that you already made the management decision about the program and you had to justify your decision to your "boss." What would you tell him or her that you saw or heard that led you to making the decision that you did? If there is not an evaluation question for that information, maybe you need to include one in your evaluation design.

If Evaluation Includes Question "What Is Progress toward Achieving Outcomes?"

To identify what information is needed to answer this evaluation question, you must identify indicators for each outcome target, if you have not yet done so. PART II provides guidelines to complete a logic model, including guidelines to identify desired outcomes for clients participating in the program, associated outcomes targets and indicators (or measures) of progress towards achievement of each outcome target.

 In the worksheet, "Planning Your Program Evaluation," in Appendix D, on the sheet titled, "Outcome Measurement Framework," write in the indicators associated with each outcome target. Note that you will need to make copies of that worksheet for each outcome.

For Other Evaluation Questions

 In the worksheet, "Planning Your Program Evaluation," in Appendix D, on the sheet titled, "Evaluation Questions and Data Collection," fill in the information needed to answer each question. Note that you need to make copies of that worksheet for each evaluation question.

What Are Best Sources for This Information/Data?

A wide variety of sources might be useful, depending on the questions that must be answered by your evaluation. Consider:

- Records/documentation

- Staff/employees

- Board members

- Clients/customers

- Funders/Investors

- Other(s)

If Evaluation Includes Question "What Is Progress toward Achieving Outcomes?"

In the worksheet, "Planning Your Program Evaluation," in Appendix D, in the section, "Outcome Measurement Framework," write in the data sources associated with each indicator. Note that you will likely have made copies of that sheet for each outcome.

For Other Evaluation Questions

In the worksheet, "Planning Your Program Evaluation," in Appendix D, in the section, "Evaluation Questions and Data Collection," fill in the data sources. Note that you will likely have made copies of that sheet for each evaluation question.

What Are Best Methods to Collect Information/Data?

The overall goal in selecting data collection method(s) is to get the most useful information to answer your evaluation questions and do so in the most cost-effective and realistic fashion. At this point, you may benefit from reading the business research information in Appendix E.

What Are Best Data Collection Tools?

Consider the following questions:

1. Of the information needed to answer the evaluation questions, how much can be collected and analyzed in a low-cost and practical manner, for example, by using questionnaires, surveys and checklists?

2. How accurate will the information be?

3. Will the data collection methods get all of the needed information?

4. What additional data collection methods should and could be used if additional information is needed?

5. Will the information be perceived as credible by decision makers, for example, by funders or top management?

6. Will the nature of the audience conform to the data collection methods, for example, will they fill out questionnaires carefully, engage in interviews or focus groups, or let you examine their documentations?

Ideally, the evaluator uses a combination of data collection methods, for example, a questionnaire to quickly collect a great deal of information from a lot of people, and then interviews to get more in-depth information from certain respondents to the questionnaires. Perhaps case studies could then be used for more in-depth analysis of unique and notable cases, for example, those who benefited or did not benefit from the program or those who quit the program.

When Is Information Needed?

For example, do you need to:

- Provide a report to a funder by a certain date?

- Provide a report to the Board by a certain date?

- Make changes to the program by a certain date?

- Generate advertising and promotions materials by a certain date?

Who Will Collect Data?

Often, this decision depends on:

- Who has access to the sources of data?

- Who has the time to collect the data?

- Who understands the data collection methods to collect the data?

- Who can administer the data collection methods? Now or is training required?

Ideally, the program has access to an "outside" evaluator who is not part of the program staff. That approach increases the likelihood that the collection of data will be done with less bias than if done by a member of the program staff. However, nonprofits often cannot afford to pay an outside evaluator to collect information.

If Evaluation Includes Question "What Is Progress toward Achieving Outcomes?"

 In the worksheet, "Planning Your Program Evaluation," in Appendix D, complete the sheet titled, "Outcome Measurement Framework," by writing in the data collection methods associated with each data source. You will need to make copies of that worksheet for each outcome.

For Other Evaluation Questions

 In the worksheet, "Planning Your Program Evaluation," in Appendix D, complete the sheet titled, "Evaluation Questions and Data collection," by filling in the data collection methods associated with each data source. Make copies of that worksheet for each evaluation question.

How Will You Analyze and Interpret Your Results?

Often, when analyzing data, there are certain indications that seem to stand out right away from the data. For example, most program participants believe the program is very good or the program seems confusing to most of your program staff. A primary goal in your analysis should be to notice all of the major indications. Usually this is not hard to do. Analyzing quantitative and qualitative data is often the topic of advanced research and evaluation. However, there are certain basic guidelines that can help you to organize and make conclusions from lots of data. Those guidelines are described in this section. Trust that you can analyze your results to the extent that you can notice what is important and what is not. You can do it.

Always Start with Your Evaluation Questions in Mind

When analyzing data (whether from questionnaires, interviews, focus groups, or whatever), always start from review of your evaluation questions. The data was collected to answer those questions in the first place, so the questions will help you organize your data and focus your analysis. For example, if you wanted to know if the program was working well or not then you can organize data into program strengths, weaknesses and suggestions to improve the program. Or, if you wanted to fully understand what activities were occurring in the program, you could organize data in the chronological order in which the program occurs. Or, if you are conducting an outcomes evaluation, you could categorize data according to the indicators for each outcome.

Basic Analysis of Quantitative Information

Quantitative data is data other than commentary, for example, ratings, rankings, yes's and no's. This type of data can be rather straightforward to organize and analyze.

1. Make copies of your data and store the master copy away in a safe place. Use the copy for making edits, cutting and pasting, etc.

2. Tabulate the information, adding up the number of ratings, rankings, yes's, no's for each question from your questionnaire or interview guide.

3. For ratings and rankings, consider computing a mean, or average, for each question. For example, "For question #1, the average ranking was 2.4." This is more meaningful than indicating, for example, how many respondents ranked 1, 2, or 3.

4. Consider conveying the range of answers, for example, 20 people ranked "1," 30 ranked "2," and 20 people ranked "3".

5. Keep all commentary for several years after completion in case needed for future reference.

Basic Analysis of Qualitative Information

Qualitative data includes commentary (they are not ratings or rankings), such as thoughts and opinions provided by people during interviews or focus groups.

1. Make copies of your data and store the master copy away in a safe place. Use the copy for making edits, cutting and pasting, etc.

2. Read through all the data.

3. Then re-read to organize comments into similar categories, for example, concerns, suggestions, strengths, weaknesses, similar experiences, program inputs, recommendations, outputs or outcome indicators.

4. Label the categories or themes, for example, concerns and suggestions.

5. Attempt to identify patterns, or associations and causal relationships in the themes, for example, all people who attended programs in the evening had similar concerns, most people came from the same geographic area, most people were in the same salary range, or what processes or events respondents experience during the program.

6. Keep all commentary for several years after completion in case needed for future reference.

Interpreting Information

Attempt to put the information in perspective, for example, compare results to:

- What you expected, or to promised results

- Any common standards for your services

- Original program goals

- Indications of accomplishing outcomes

- Description of the program's experiences, strengths, weaknesses, etc.

Consider especially any recommendations to help program staff improve the program, conclusions about program operations or meeting goals, etc.

How Will You Report Your Evaluation Results?

You will need to document your program evaluation results, with conclusions and recommendations, in a written document. You should also associate interpretations to justify your conclusions or recommendations. The level and scope of the content of the report depends on for whom the report is intended, for example, bankers, funders, employees, customers, clients or the public.

Be sure employees have a chance to carefully review and discuss the report. Translate recommendations to action plans, including who is going to do what about the program and by when.

Bankers or funders will likely require a report that includes:

- An executive summary

- Description of the organization and the program under evaluation

- Explanation of the evaluation goals, data collection methods, and analysis procedures

- Listing of conclusions and recommendations

- Any relevant attachments, for example, evaluation questionnaires or interview guides

The funder may want the report to be delivered as a presentation, accompanied by an overview of the report. Or, the funder may want to review the report alone.

> PART IV includes guidelines to assemble and implement an evaluation plan.

> In the worksheet, "Planning Your Program Evaluation," in Appendix D, fill in the section "How will the evaluation results be reported, including to whom?"

Who Should Conduct the Evaluation?

Ideally, management decides what the evaluation goals should be. Then an evaluation expert helps the organization to determine what the evaluation design should be, and how the resulting data will be analyzed and reported back to the organization. Most organizations do not have the resources to conduct the ideal evaluation.

Still, they can make the 20% of effort needed to generate the 80% of what they need to know to make a decision about a program. If they can afford any outside help, it should be to select the appropriate evaluation design, including how to collect data. The organization might find a less expensive resource to apply the data collection methods, for example, conduct interviews, or send out and analyze results of questionnaires.

If no outside help can be obtained, the organization can still learn a great deal by applying the data collection methods and analyzing results themselves. However, there is a strong chance that data about the strengths and weaknesses of a program will not be interpreted fairly if that information is analyzed by the people responsible for the program – program managers will be "policing" themselves. This caution is not to fault program managers, but to recognize the strong biases inherent in trying to objectively look at and publicly (at least within the organization) report about their programs. Therefore, if possible, have someone other than the program managers look at and determine evaluation results.

> In the worksheet, "Planning Your Program Evaluation," in Appendix D, fill in the section "Who should conduct the evaluation?"

Review and Test Evaluation Plans

If you have been following the guidelines in the section, "Guidelines for Successful Program Development and Evaluation," in PART I, you conducted your evaluation planning by using a team of people in your organization and you made sure that they included their perspectives on the planning activities and results.

Many times your initial program evaluation plans will change, sometimes substantially during implementation of the plans. That is okay. The point is to recognize the need for the change, what needs to be changed and how, update the plans and then communicate the updated plans to all organization members affected by the plan.

Many experts in evaluation assert that your evaluation plans should go through a preliminary "test run" to be sure that they are understandable, useful and accurate. However, many small- to medium-sized nonprofits simply do not have the resources to conduct a test run of their evaluation plans. But they can consider the first application of the evaluation plans – for example, during the first year of the program – to be the test run. To do this, program planners must carefully monitor implementation of the evaluation plan – and the evaluation planning itself – to polish the evaluation plans, including the identification of the evaluation questions, information needed to answer the questions, methods to collect information, and the analysis and reporting of the evaluation results.

Ethics and Information Privacy

Participants of programs that are being evaluated are, in effect, research participants. Research participants deserve to have the choice to participate in research activities, especially as to how any information about them might be used. Therefore, it is important to ensure they have this clear choice and that their choice is clearly documented. The following paragraphs might be considered as policy regarding confidentially in your program evaluation, and for inclusion as terms in an information-release form to be used in your program evaluation, as well.

- Any identifiable information in regard to use of a participant's name, name of their agency, and reference to their goals and activities in their program will *not* be mentioned by anyone outside the program, including by evaluators, program staff, etc., either verbally or in *any* publication now or in the future, without express, written consent of the program participant.

- All participants in the evaluation will sign an information-release form that conveys their express written consent toward terms of their participation in the evaluation, including use of their name, name of their agency, and reference to their goals and activities carried out in their program. A sample Information Release Form is in the Appendix E of this document.

Pitfalls to Avoid During Evaluation Planning

Regardless of the type of evaluation that you conduct, you should pay careful attention to avoid the following pitfalls.

1. **Do not balk at evaluation because it seems far too "scientific."**
   It is not. Usually the first 20% of effort will generate the first 80% of a good evaluation, and this is far better than nothing.

2. **There is no "perfect" evaluation design**.
   Do not worry about the plan being perfect. It is far more important to do something that seems reasonable for now, than to wait until every detail has been tested.

3. **Work hard to include some interviews in your data collection methods**. Questionnaires do not capture "the story," and the story is usually the most powerful depiction of the benefits of your services.

4.   **Do not interview just the successes**.
        You will learn a great deal about the program by understanding its failures, drop-outs, etc.

5.   **Do not throw away evaluation results once a report has been generated**.
        Results do not take up much room, and they can provide precious information later when trying to understand changes in the program.

PART IV:

ASSEMBLING AND

IMPLEMENTING PLANS

Role of Leadership

Organizations often undertake comprehensive planning activities that generate descriptive plan documents – but the plans are rarely opened at all. Guidelines in the section, "Guidelines to Ensure Successful Planning and Implementation," in PART I, explain how planners can increase the likelihood that their plans will be implemented.

However, no matter how comprehensive or specific the guidelines about implementation, plans will likely not be implemented unless leaders in the organization persuade others to actually implement the plans. Leadership is setting direction and influencing others to follow that direction. Leaders set direction, usually in the form of well-written plans. The rest of the responsibilities of leadership are to ensure that the plans are utilized.

Sometimes members of organizations are "turned off" by planning and plans because they have seen far too many planning sessions result in lots of discussion, but little action. Leadership on accountability, supported by a strong implementation plan, can turn that perception around.

Sometimes they are turned off because they believe that plans too quickly become out-of-date and are much too restrictive. That belief comes from the impression that plans are somehow absolute rules that must be followed no matter what happens. That is a mistaken impression. Plans are guidelines. They can be changed and often should be changed. The point is to recognize the need for the change, clarify what changes should be made and why, and then widely communicate the changes to members who are interested in the plan.

Perhaps the strongest benefit of a good plan is providing a common frame of reference around which members of the organization can communicate. In that case, members should continue to reference the plan document. It should not just sit collecting dust on a shelf. That problem can be avoided if the executive leadership does its job.

To learn more about leadership, see the annotated list of resources on page 246.

Assembling Plans

One of the best ways to ensure that an organization realizes the results of effective planning is to record the planning results in the form of an overall plan document. This section provides guidelines and suggested formats to assemble a variety of plans.

If you have been completing the various worksheets in Appendix D that correspond to each of the topics in PART II and III, you have completed most, if not all, of the contents that you need to assemble into the plans described in this section.

Sections Common to Many Plan Documents

The contents and format of a plan document ultimately depend on the purpose of the document and the audience that will use the plan. However, most major plan documents have many sections in common. You should consider assembling these common sections into whatever plan you choose to create. The final format of each of your plans is suggested in the following sections.

Common sections of plan documents include:

Cover Sheet

Information on the cover sheet usually specifies:

- Title of the plan.

- Name of the organization that produced the plan.

- Whether the plan is in draft status or not
  (draft status indicates that the contents are not yet finished and approved).

- Date the plan was assembled or updated.

- Any restrictions on access to the contents (if access should be limited to certain groups). Consider indicating this level of propriety on every page of the plan, as well.

Table of Contents

The Table of Contents lists the major sections and subsections of the plan and includes the page numbers of each section and subsection.

Authorization Sheet

This page includes indication that the plan has been, or will be, approved. The page might include, for example:

- Explanation of the level of authorization, for example, "This plan is subject to approval by the Board of Directors as recommend by the Board Program Committee. Approval is indicated by the Board member signatures below."

- Blank lines on which the approval can be indicated in the form of written signatures and dates next to those signatures.

Executive Summary

The Executive Summary is sometimes misunderstood to be similar to the Table of Contents. The Executive Summary should not be merely a summary listing of the contents of the plan (that is a Table of Contents), but rather a succinct description of the highlights of the plan. The Summary should include information such that Board members, executive management and sometimes external stakeholders, such as funders, can scan the Summary to grasp:

- The purpose of the plan, including how the plan will be used and any overall results expected from implementing the plan.

- Who was primarily responsible for the development of the plan.

- When implementation of the plan will be started and completed.

- Who is ultimately responsible for the implementation of the plan.

- Any key highlights or issues discovered during planning and recommendations to address the issues.

- Any specific actions currently required from any specific groups, such as approval by the Board.

- How implementation of the plan will be monitored.

The Executive Summary should usually be no more than one to two pages in length.

Body of Plan

The content and format of the body of the plan depend on the nature of the plan, for example, whether it is a strategic plan, business plan, marketing plan, evaluation plan, etc. This section often includes:

- Description of the organization that produced or will use the plan, including its major products or services; top-level, strategic "philosophy," such as mission, vision and values; and its major interest or intent for the plan

- Description of the plan's goals and strategies to achieve the goals

- Description of any action planning or implementation planning to ensure the goals are achieved on time, including specification of who will do what and by when, and what resources they need to do it

The contents of the body of the report will likely correspond to some, or all, of the terms in the section, "Basic Planning Process and Terms," in PART I.

The following sections describe what might be in the body of a particular plan in more detail.

Appendices

Appendices often include information and materials that are supplementary, or in addition to, the key points of the plan. Appendices often include:

- Explanation of how the plan was developed

- Data generated from analyses associated with the plan, for example, environmental scans and market research

- Financials associated with obtaining and supporting use of the expertise and materials required to implement the plan

- Listing of any related or supporting documents, such as related plans, reports, etc.

Assembling Program Development Plan

The development plan describes the tasks, expertise and materials needed to build the program "from the ground up." In addition to the contents listed in the previous section, "Sections Common to Many Plan Documents," development plans usually include the following information listed below. Ultimately, the nature of the format and content of the program development plan is up to the organization that develops and will use the plan.

Note that if you have followed the guidelines in PART II, you will have already completed much of what is required for a development plan.

1. Purpose of plan

2. Description of service and project to build service

   a) Conceptual model (logic model)

   b) Description of service (name, forms and formats)

   c) Overview of tasks, expertise and materials

   d) Project development plan and schedules

3. Required tasks (general steps to build service)

   a) Build service (prototype, marketing materials, documentation, etc.)

   b) Test/Pilot service

   c) Finish design and build of service

4. Required expertise (staffing plan)

   a) Assignments and roles (job descriptions)

   b) Staffing (hiring and training)

c) Organization and management (organization plan, policies and procedures)

5.   Required materials

a) Tools

b) Supplies

c) Equipment

d) Facilities

6.   Financials

a) Capital budget, if applicable (costs to purchase facilities and large equipment, etc.) (Note that this Field Guide does not provide guidelines to design a capital budget.)

> For more information about designing a capital budget, see the topic, "Basic Guide to Nonprofit Financial Management," at http://www.managementhelp.org/finance/np_fnce/np_fnce.htm.

b) Program budget (personnel, tools, supplies, etc.)

> The preceding section, "Sections Common to Many Plan Documents," suggests several items to include in the appendices of a plan.

Assembling Program Marketing Plan

The marketing plan pulls together all of the highlights from the marketing analysis, and adds specific marketing goals with timelines. In addition to the contents listed in the previous section, "Sections Common to Many Plan Documents," marketing plans usually also include the following information. Ultimately, the nature of the format and content of the marketing plan is up to the organization that develops and will use the plan.

Note that if you have followed the guidelines in PART II, you will have already completed much of what is required for a marketing plan.

1.   Purpose of plan

2.   Marketing goals and any brief, associated commentary about each goal

3.   Description of service, including:

a) The name of your service

b) What the service provides

c) The specific target markets and the benefits of the program to each of them

    d) The price(s) of your program

    e) How clients can pay

    f) Forms and formats (packaging) in which the program is provided

4. Remaining tasks and considerations that might be necessary to complete the marketing analysis

5. Implementation section that specifies:

    a) Each marketing goal and/or other tasks to accomplish good marketing

    b) Who is responsible to address each goal or do each task

    c) Deadline for achievement of the goal or completion of the task

    d) Specification of any monies budgeted to obtain and support resources to achieve the goal or do the task

Assembling Program Promotions Plans (Sales, Advertising and Promotions)

These plans describe the overall promotions campaign that will be regularly conducted by the program to ensure that the target markets are fully aware of, and take advantage of, the program's services. In addition to the contents listed in the previous section, "Sections Common to Many Plan Documents," advertising, promotions and sales plans usually also include the following information listed below. Ultimately, the nature of the format and content of the program promotions plans are up to the organization that develops and will use the plans.

Note that if you have followed the guidelines in PART II, you will have already completed much of what is required for advertising, promotions and sales plans.

Advertising and Promotions Plan

1. Purpose of plan

2. Approach to each target market, including:

    a) Description of target market

    b) Unique value proposition

    c) Key features and benefits of program to that market

    d) Key message(s) to convey

    e) Methods/tools to convey message(s)

3.   Remaining tasks and considerations that might be necessary to complete the advertising and promotions analysis

4.   Implementation section that specifies:

    a)   Who is responsible to advertise to each target market

    b)   Who is responsible to attend to any remaining tasks and considerations

    c)   Deadline by which advertising and tasks should be addressed

    d)   Specification of funds budgeted to obtain and support advertising resources

Sales Plan

1.   Purpose of plan

2.   Sales approach to each target market, including:

    a)   How to generate leads (resulting from advertising, etc.)

    b)   How to conduct follow-ups to leads (gain opportunities to conduct presentations, etc.)

    c)   How to close sales (accomplish formal contracting for services)

3.   Remaining tasks and considerations that might be necessary to complete the sales planning and analysis

4.   Implementation section that specifies:

    a)   Who is responsible to sell to each target market

    b)   Who is responsible to attend to any remaining tasks and considerations

    c)   Deadlines for any key sales activities and attending to tasks

    d)   Specification of funds budgeted to obtain and support sales resources

Assembling Program Operations Plan

The operations plan describes the ongoing activities that must be carried out to continue to deliver the program directly to its target markets. The activities are directly in regard to delivering services to clients, rather than, for example, operating all of the organization and its other programs. Some organizations prefer to format the plan in the form of an operations manual that can be referenced by staff to operate the program. In addition to the contents listed in the previous section, "Sections Common to Many Plan Documents," an operations plan usually also includes the information listed below. Ultimately, the nature of the format and content of an operations plan is up to the organization that develops and will use the plan.

Note that if you have followed the guidelines in PART II, you will have already completed much of what is required for a program operations plan.

1.   Purpose of plan

2.   Program service delivery functions (direct contact and service to clients):

    a)   Client intake, registration

     b)   Client servicing

     c)   Client exit from program

3.   Program administrative functions:

     a)   Purchase supplies and equipment

     b)   Office administration (office supplies, property management, clerical support, etc.)

     c)   Bookkeeping and accounting (information management)

     d)   Financial analysis (report generation and analysis)

     e)   Computer system administration

     f)   Produce service/product (reproduce resources required for direct delivery of services)

     g)   Advertising and promotion

     h)   Sales and customer service

     i)   Professional services (lawyers, bankers, accountants, etc.)

In the operations plan, be sure to include:

4.   Program services documentation

     a)   Forms, procedures, checklists, etc., used to deliver services to clients

     b)   Policies and procedures regarding delivery of services

5.   Program staffing plan (see next section)

Assembling Program Staffing Plan

The staffing plan describes the personnel, or human resources, necessary to operate the program. In addition to the contents listed in the previous section, "Sections Common to Many Plan Documents," a program staffing plan usually also includes the following information listed below. Ultimately, the nature of the format and content of a staffing plan is up to the organization that develops and will use the plan.

Note that if you have followed the guidelines in PART II, you will have already completed much of what is required for a program staffing plan.

1.   Purpose of plan

2.   Assignments and roles to provide service:

     a)   Listing of required roles to provide service (part-time, full-time, and volunteers)

     b)   Roles and responsibilities for each role (job descriptions)

3.   Staffing

     a)   Hiring plan (job descriptions, recruiting and screening procedures)

     b)   Volunteer recruiting procedures

  c) Training plans (how staff and volunteers will be trained to provide the service)

4.   Organization and management

  a) Organization plan (organization chart)

  b) Related personnel policies and procedures

In the staffing plan, you might also include:

5.   Staffing budgets that include funds for making staff productive, for example:

  a) Salaries

  b) Wages

  c) Fringe benefits

  d) Training

  e) Professional memberships

  f) Travel

Assembling Nonprofit Business Plan

You should consider a nonprofit business plan for a nonprofit program under any of the following conditions:

- The nature of the new program is new to your organization.

- You will need funding to develop and operate the program.

- You are not very familiar with the program's clients and their needs.

- You are not completely sure how to meet their needs.

A comprehensive, well-written fundraising proposal is similar, and sometimes the same as, a business plan. Consequently, if you submit a grant proposal that is as complete as a business plan, you might increase your chances of getting funded. More than most types of plans, the nature of the format and content of a business plan is ultimately up to the audience that will use the business plan, including the organization that develops and will use the plan. There are a variety of formats of business plans. In addition to the contents listed in the previous section, "Sections Common to Many Plan Documents," business plans might include the following information listed below.

Note that if you have followed the guidelines in PART II, you will have already completed much of what is required in a nonprofit business plan. Items that are not addressed in this Field Guide are marked as such below.

Part One: Description of Organization and Product or Service

1.   Description of the product or service, including descriptions of:

   a)   The clients' need that will be addressed by the new program, including brief mention of research results that substantiate the existence of the need

   b)   The methods that the program will use to meet the need, including brief mention of research results that substantiate the selection of program methods

   c)   Name of the product or service

   d)   Pricing and packaging of the product or service

   e)   How clients will pay

2.   Overview of the market, including:

   a)   The overall market and the specific target markets that will be served

   b)   How large the target markets are

   c)   Trends about the target markets that suggest increasing need for your program

   d)   Why they will be motivated to use your program

   e)   How many clients you expect to serve and over what time period

3.   Overview of marketing plans, including:

   a)   How you determined your pricing and packaging

   b)   Sales, marketing and advertising strategies

   c)   How you will ensure high quality services

4.   Description of the organization's competition:

   a)   Who your competitors are

   b)   What they provide and what they charge

   c)   Why you are starting a program that competes with theirs

5.   Highlights of financials, specifically:

   a)   What you expect to earn from fees for services

   b)   What the product will cost to produce/deliver

   c)   How you expect to make up for any differences if expenses exceed revenues

6. Description of the management and personnel resources, including:

    a) What management resources will be applied

    b) How they will be organized

    c) Qualifications of current management

    d) What personnel are needed

    e) What they will do

    f) How they will be recruited and trained

    g) What they will be paid

Part Two: Financial Requirements

1. Explanation of the funding that is sought, including:

    a) The amount requested and when you need it

    b) How that amount was derived

    c) How it will be spent

    d) Your organization's monetary contribution to the effort

    e) How the program will become self-sustaining over time, if it will

    f) What you will do if you do not get the money

2. Program development budget (include this budget if you are applying for money to build the program "from the ground up"), including:

    a) Expenses to obtain personnel and materials

    b) Expenses to pay personnel to develop the program

3. Program operating budget, or depiction of monies to operate the program:

    a) Expected expenses

    b) Expected revenues

4. Program's capital budget, or depiction of monies needed for purchase of large, long-lasting assets, such as facilities and equipment. This budget is basically a listing of the items and the expected cost of each.

5.   Break-even analysis that depicts when the program will start making more money than it is spending (if that will ever be the case). Funders are often reluctant to fund programs that will continue to operate with large deficits. (Note that this Field Guide did not provide guidelines to produce a break-even analysis.)

6.   Cash flow projection that shows how much money the program will have coming in (revenues), usually depicted for at least each month of the coming year, and the amounts of money going out (expenses), usually depicted for at least each month of the coming year. (Note that this Field Guide did not provide guidelines to design a cash budget.)

> For more information about producing a break-even analysis or a cash budget, see the topic, "Basic Guide to Nonprofit Financial Management" at http://www.managementhelp.org/finance/np_fnce/np_fnce.htm.

Part Three: Organization

1.   Information about the organization, in particular, to show why the program is well worth the investment from the funder. Include:

   a)   Mission and relationship of the proposed program to the mission

   b)   Current programs

   c)   History

   d)   Major accomplishments

   e)   Strengths (for example, good financial and program management) and suitability to develop and provide the proposed program

2.   Organization's financial statements, including: (Note that the terms "Statements of ..." are used in the USA. Various countries might have their own preferred types of financial statements and names for these statements. The terms "balance sheet," "income statement" and "cash budget" are commonly used in the USA and Canada.)

   a)   Statement of Financial Position (balance sheets) at least for the past year

   b)   Statement of Financial Activities (income statements) at least for the past year

   c)   Cash budget (depicting expected cash flow over coming year)

> For more information on cash budgets and other financial matters, see the topic, "Basic Guide to Nonprofit Financial Management," at http://www.managementhelp.org/finance/np_fnce/np_fnce.htm. (Note that this Field Guide does not provide guidelines on generating and analyzing the above three financial statements.)

Part Four: Any Supporting Documents

There can be any variety of supporting documents, depending on the nature of the program and the expectations of the funder. For example, you might include:

1.   Resumes of the senior management

2.   Official estimates of the costs of equipment that would be purchased with the funds

3.   Market data that substantiates the program's claim that the product or service is in strong demand

Assembling Program Evaluation Plan

Ultimately, the nature of the format and content of an evaluation plan is up to the organization that develops and will use the plan. In addition to the contents listed in the previous section, "Sections Common to Many Plan Documents," program evaluation plans usually also include the following information listed below.

Note that if you have followed the guidelines in PART III, you will have already completed much of what is required in a program evaluation plan.

1.   Purpose of the report, including what type of evaluation(s) are, or were to be, conducted; what decisions are being aided by the findings of the evaluation; who is making the decision and on what basis

2.   Description of program's primary service that is being evaluated, including:

   a) The community need(s) that it helps to meet

   b) Overall vision and goals of the program

   c) Desired outcomes for participants in the program

   d) Methods that the program uses to achieve its vision and goals

   e) Staffing utilized to implement the methods

3.   Overall evaluation questions that are intended to be answered by the evaluation

4.   Methodology of the evaluation

   a) Types of data/information that were collected

   b) How data/information were collected (what instruments were used, etc.)

   c) How data/information were analyzed

   d) Limitations of the evaluation (cautions about any findings/conclusions and how to use the findings/conclusions, etc.)

5.   Interpretations and conclusions (from analysis of the data/information)

6.   Recommendations (regarding the program decisions that must be made about the program)

In the program evaluation plan, you might also include the following appendices:

7.   Instruments used to collect data/information

8.   Data, often in tabular format; try to include only the data that is directly related to answering an evaluation question

9.   Testimonials and key comments made by users of the product/service/program

10.   Case studies of key users of the program

11.   Any related literature

Assembling Fundraising Proposal

A fundraising proposal is a written, formal solicitation to a funder to obtain funds for a project, often a program. Ideally, a nonprofit organization includes proposal planning in the overall context of a total fundraising plan. Overall, a fundraising plan includes specification of fundraising goals, specific sources of funds, how to approach those funders, who will approach the funders and how.

For more information about fundraising, see the annotated list of resources on page 245.

As noted previously in this Field Guide, a well-written fundraising proposal includes a description of a well-designed program plan, and a well-designed program plan is essentially the same as a well-designed nonprofit business plan, one of the major outcomes from using this Field Guide. Thus, if you have been following the guidelines in this Field Guide, you have already developed most of what would be in a well-written fundraising proposal.

However, the standard format of a fundraising proposal is usually somewhat different from the format of the other plans described in this section about assembling plans. The format of a proposal to a certain funder ultimately depends on the format desired by the funder, which is usually specified by the funder in their grant guidelines. Nonprofits can obtain those guidelines by contacting the funder.

The standard format of a fundraising proposal is often according to the following format.

Note that, although it is not within the scope of this Field Guide to provide guidelines and materials to design and implement a complete fundraising plan, if you have followed the guidelines in PART II, you will have already completed much of what is required for a fundraising proposal.

1.   Cover letter, including brief:

        a) Description of the request for funding

        b) Purpose of the funding

    c) Description of the organization making the solicitation

    d) How the organization will follow-up (for example, calling or requesting a visit)

    e) Signature of the Chief Executive Officer and relevant member of the Board of Directors

2. Executive summary, including:

    a) Description of the request for funding

    b) Overview of the community need to be met by the program

    c) Description of how the program will meet the need

    d) Mention of planned schedules for program activities (for example, development, pilot testing or first program evaluation)

    e) Explanation of the time period of the program to be funded by the donor (for example, program development or program operations during years)

    f) Explanation of why the donation is a good investment for the funder

    g) Mention of how follow-up will be conducted (for example, the funder will be called)

3. Background information, including description of the requesting nonprofit's:

    a) Mission and relationship of the proposed program to the mission

    b) Current programs

    c) History

    d) Major accomplishments

    e) Strengths (for example, good financial and program management) and suitability to develop and provide the proposed program

4. Needs statement (or problem statement), including description of:

    a) Community's need, including its nature and size

    b) Evidence of the need (include quantifiable research data, not only anecdotes and opinions)

    c) Mention of the types of research that you conducted to generate the evidence

    d) Criticality of meeting the need

    e) Which part of the need your program aims to meet

5. Vision and goals, including:

   a) Depiction of how the community will be operating after the need has been met (your program vision)

   b) Goals in terms of impacts on clients (outcomes, or outcomes targets if they exist) and written to be SMART, including deadlines for achieving goals

   c) Goals in terms of activities of the program (for example, "develop a model program that can be duplicated elsewhere") and written to be SMART, including deadlines for achieving goals

   d) Explanation of how the vision and goals are directly associated with meeting the needs of the community

6. Methods, including description of:

   a) What major activities (methods) will be conducted to meet the community need

   b) What research was conducted to select the methods (includes research data, not only anecdotes and opinions)

   c) How the methods are directly associated with meeting the need

   d) Any other efforts in the community that operate to meet the particular need that is also meant to be addressed by the program

   e) Resources that currently exist and do not exist (so they have to be obtained) within the nonprofit organization

   f) What resources (people and materials) are needed by the nonprofit to implement the methods

7. Evaluation methodology (see "Assembling Program Evaluation Plan"), including:

   a) Evaluation questions that will be addressed by the program evaluation

   b) Types of data/information that will be collected

   c) How the data/information will be collected

   d) How the data/information will be analyzed

   e) How the data/information will be reported

8. Future funding, including:

   a) Sources from which funding will be sought (individuals, foundations, corporations and/or government)

   b) What amounts from what sources

c) When the sources will be approached

9.   Program budget that depicts expected financial information for the time period relevant to the proposal, and including:

a) Expenses to develop the program (if the proposal is in regard to developing the program)

b) Expenses for direct costs to operate the program, including people (salaries and fringe), materials (supplies, equipment, facilities), utilities, training, etc.

c) Expenses for indirect (overhead) costs to operate the program, including for support of any people, materials, etc., that are used to support other programs or parts of the organization other than those used by the proposed program

d) Revenue from fees and fundraising (donations, in-kind donations)

10.   Appendices, including:

a) Research results that verified existence of need, program methods to meet need, etc. (include summaries, if possible)

b) Copy of the nonprofit's strategic plan

c) Nonprofit's financial reports, including Statement of Financial Position, Statement of Financial Activities, and cash budget (note that various countries might prefer their own types of reports, including the names for these reports, as well)

d) Testimonials about the strengths of the nonprofit

e) The nonprofit's official designation of charitable status (for example, in the USA, the IRS letter of determination; in Canada, designation from the Canada Customs and Revenue Agency)

f) List of the current members of the Board of Directors

Have Plans Reviewed By Others

One of the most important lessons that new planners learn is to have some people, other than the planners, review the plan document. Until the plan has been reviewed, it should be considered a "draft" and marked as such on the title of the plan.

Reviewers should consider the following aspects of the document:

- **Coherency of the organization of contents**
  Are the major contents arranged in an understandable manner?

- **Completeness**
  Is the plan complete? Are all necessary aspects of the planning process and results in the plan?

- **Clarity**
  Do the format and wording make sense?

- **Direction**
  Is it clear what the plan requires to be done and in what order?

- **Practicality**
  Can the plan be implemented in a reasonable fashion?

- **Accountability**
  Is it clear who is to implement the plan? Is it clear how the implementation of the plan will be tracked? Is it clear who is ultimately responsible for the implementation of the plan?

Approve Final Version of Plans

One of the most important criteria to ensure the success of the implementation of a plan is to ensure that the plan has the full approval and support of the Board and management. Therefore, it is important to have the plan, at least its highlights, reviewed and approved by upper management. The plan can be reviewed by a Board committee, for example, a Programs Committee or Marketing Committee, which makes a recommendation to the full Board regarding the acceptance of the plan.

One of the major responsibilities of the Board of Directors is to ensure that the nonprofit has clear strategic direction and that the nonprofit and its programs follow that strategic direction. One of the best ways for the Board to carry out this responsibility is through coordinating the development and implementation of plans, including strategic plans, business plans, program development, marketing plans and program evaluation plans. Therefore, the Board should review and approve major plans.

Implementing Plans

Tools to Track Status of Implementation

If the program was designed well, processes in the program should regularly generate information that indicates the status of the implementation of the plan.

Implementation Section in Plans

One of the most important tools in this regard is the Implementation Section of the plan. That section specifies:

1.   What specific goals or tasks must be addressed to implement the plan

2.   Who is responsible to address each goal or task

3.   By when (a deadline)

4.   What resources, usually in terms of funding, that the person needs to address the goal or task by the deadline

Regular, Written Status Reports

Written status reports should be provided on a regular basis, perhaps weekly during development of the program and monthly during operation of a program. Reports should be dated and describe:

1.   What activities were done over the past time period

2.   Any current actions or issues that must be addressed by management

3.   Plans for activities on the next time period

Program managers can monitor implementation of the plan by enforcing the terms laid out in the Implementation Section.

Program Reviews and Key Questions to Ask

Program implementation reviews are regular examinations of the program's development activities to assess how well the program is developing. A program development review team should probably include the Chief Executive Officer, the head of the new program and one or two other program directors, particularly those from programs that closely coordinate with the new program. Examine if the program seems to be following the original plan. If it is not, the deviation is not as important as understanding why and assessing if the deviation was necessary. Look at key indicators, such as:

1.   What major problems exist and what is needed to address them?

2.   How are the actual costs compared to the planned costs?

3.   Are any actions needed to avoid financial problems?

4.   What would you do differently about the program if you could do anything?

5.   What limitations are holding you back from what you would ideally do if you could?

6.   What are you learning from the program implementation so far?

7.   How are you acknowledging and celebrating the accomplishments?

Capture Learnings from Implementation of Plans

Adults learn best by applying new information and materials to real-world challenges and by exchanging feedback with others. Implementation of plans involves both of these ideal conditions for learning. Thus, when implementing plans, stay focused on what you are learning. The following table depicts some of the potential areas of learnings for you and how you might use them.

Your learnings from addressing:	Can be applied to update/improve:
Any planning process	Quality of any planning that you do, i.e., strategic planning, program planning, etc.
Marketing and operations planning	Update the description of the program, including the logic model
Marketing goals	Advertising, promotions, sales
Advertising, promotions, sales planning	Marketing goals
Materials planning	Capital budgeting
Development planning	Development budgeting
Operations planning	Operating budget
Program evaluation, including: - Goals evaluation - Implementation evaluation - Process evaluation - Outcomes evaluation	Marketing goals Outcomes in Logic Model Methods in Logic Model
Reviewing processes of developing plans and of implementing plan	Improve planning processes, i.e., program planning and program evaluation planning

APPENDICES

Appendix A: Key Terms

Appendix B: Resources for Nonprofits

Appendix C: Checklist of Nonprofit Management Indicators

Appendix D: Worksheets

Appendix E: Basic Methods in Business Research

Appendix F: Major Methods of Advertising and Promotions

Appendix A: Key Terms

Advertising

Bringing a product (or service) to the attention of potential and current customers. Advertising is typically done with signs, brochures, commercials, direct mailings or e-mail messages, personal contact, etc. See **Promotions.**

Business planning

Planning conducted when expanding a current organization, product or service. Business planning is often conducted when starting a new organization, product or service. In addition, business planning can be useful when acquiring a current organization, product or service. Business planning can even be useful when working to improve the management of a current organization, product or service. There are various formats for a business plan, which usually include at least a combination of a marketing plan, operational/management plan and a financial plan. Funders or investors usually require a business plan.

Capital budget

Depicts the money needed to obtain major, fixed assets, such as large equipment, facilities, etc.

Charity (nonprofit)

A charity (or charitable or tax-deductible nonprofit) has attained status from the appropriate government agency such that the nonprofit can receive donations and the donors can deduct the amount of donations from their tax liabilities.

Chief Executive Officer

The definition of "Chief Executive Officer" depends on whether an organization is a corporation or not, including whether it has a Board of Directors or not. In an organization that has a Board of Directors, the "Chief Executive Officer" is (usually) the singular organizational position that is primarily responsible to implement the strategic plans and policies established by the Board of Directors. In this case, the Chief Executive reports to the Board of Directors. In a form of business that is usually without a Board of Directors (sole proprietorship, etc.), the "Chief Executive Officer" is (usually) the singular organizational position that sets the direction and oversees the operations of an organization.

Corporation

An organization that is chartered (or incorporated) by the appropriate governmental agency to exist as a legal entity separate from the members of the organization. Corporations require a Board of Directors to oversee the direction and operations of the corporation. Nonprofits often are "chartered" as corporations; thus, they must have a Board of Directors. There are certain advantages to chartering an organization as a corporation, including limited liability of organization members for the operations of the organization. Also, the corporation can own property, hold its own bank account, enter into contracts, and conduct tax-exempt activities (although some countries might not require incorporation to be tax-exempt). An organization often must be incorporated to be eligible for charitable status although some countries might not require this.

Direct costs
> Expenses that are directly associated with the program and delivery of services to clients, including costs for:
> a) People who spend all their time leading, managing or providing the program and not serving other programs; and
> b) For the supplies, materials, equipment, facilities, etc., that are completely allocated to the program and not used by other programs.

Evaluation (program)
> Systematically collecting and analyzing information regarding a program to make a decision about the program.

Executive Director
> A title commonly used for the Chief Executive Officer of a nonprofit organization. See **Chief Executive Officer**.

Expenses
> The monies needed to obtain and support the resources (people, supplies, materials, etc.) required to operate the program.

Indirect costs (sometimes called "overhead")
> The expenses that are not direct costs, for example, costs for:
> a) People who lead, manage or provide resources for more than one program.
> b) Supplies, materials, equipment, facilities, etc., that are used by more than one program.
> See **Direct Costs.**

Inputs
> Items that are used by the various processes in the system to achieve the overall goal of the system. Types of inputs are people, money, equipment, facilities, supplies, people's ideas, people's time, etc.

Logic model
> A depiction of the overall conceptual "system" of a nonprofit program by depicting the inputs, processes (or activities), outputs and outcomes in regard to the program. Outcomes might be listed as short-term, intermediate or long-term.

Market research
> Carefully collecting information about various markets and aspects of markets, for example, to identify their needs, how their needs might be met, etc.

Marketing
> The wide range of activities involved in making sure that you are continuing to meet the needs of your customers and getting sufficient value in return. These activities include market research to find out, for example, what groups of potential customers exist, what their needs are, which of those needs you can meet, how you should meet them, etc. Marketing also includes analyzing the competition, positioning your new product or service (finding your market niche), pricing your products and services, and promoting them through continued advertising, promotions, public relations and sales.

Markets

Groups of potential customers/clients for a product or service. Markets might be further defined and organized by the common traits among various subgroups (target markets) such as their locale, buying habits, preferences, etc. Target markets are markets that are "targeted" by your marketing activities.

Nonprofit

A nonprofit organization exists primarily to meet a community need. An informal nonprofit is a group of people who gather to work on usually a short-term need in the community, for example, to clean up the neighborhood streets. A "chartered," or incorporated, nonprofit has filed with the appropriate government agency to be a legal entity separate from the members of the organization. A tax-exempt nonprofit has attained status from the appropriate government agency that allows the nonprofit to not have to pay certain federal and/or state (provincial in Canada) and/or local taxes. A tax-deductible nonprofit has attained status from the appropriate government agency such that the nonprofit can receive donations and the donors can deduct the amount of donations from their tax liabilities.

Outcomes

The changes, or impacts, on the clients who participated in your program. Outcomes are sometimes specified in terms of changed:
a) Knowledge, often called short-term outcomes
b) Behaviors, especially those that comprise useful skills, often called intermediate outcomes
c) Attitudes, values, conditions, etc., often called long-term outcomes

Outputs

The tangible results produced by the organization or any of its various programs. Outputs are often described by using numbers, for example, the number of clients who completed a certain program. Note that outputs (produced by the program) differ from outcomes (produced by program participants).

Processes (Activities)

Series of activities conducted by the organization or program that manipulate the various inputs to achieve the overall desired goal of the organization or program.

Program budget

A depiction of the program expenses and revenues during a specific period of program operation.

Program evaluation

Systematically collecting and analyzing information regarding a program to make a decision about the program.

Programs

Related and (hopefully) well-organized resources and methods intended to provide certain related products and/or services to a group of constituents, for example, to clients, customers, patients, etc. Nonprofits usually provide major services in the forms of programs.

Promotions

Methods to keep products in the minds of the customers and helps stimulate demand for the products. The ongoing activities of advertising, sales and public relations are often considered aspects of promotions.

Public relations

Ongoing activities to ensure the organization has a strong public image. Public relations activities include helping the public to understand the organization and its products and services. Often, public relations are conducted through the media, including newspapers, television and magazines. As noted above, public relations are often considered as one of the primary activities in promotions.

Publicity

Mention in the media. Organizations do not control the message in the media, at least not as much as they do in advertising. Reporters and writers decide what will be said, though press releases often influence what is published.

Revenue

Refers to the money earned (fees) by, or donated to, the program during operation of the program.

Sales

Involves most or many of the following activities, including cultivating prospective buyers (or leads) in a market segment; helping leads to understand how the features and benefits of a product or service can be beneficial to the lead; and closing the sale (or coming to agreement on pricing and services).

Target markets

Specific groups of potential customers/clients to whom an organization hopes to sell products or services. Consequently, the organization might focus strong efforts of market research, advertising and promotions at that specific group.

Tax-exempt (nonprofit)

A tax-exempt nonprofit has attained status from the appropriate government agency that allows the nonprofit to avoid paying certain federal and/or state (provincial in Canada) and/or local taxes.

Appendix B: Resources for Nonprofits

Free Management Library^{SM}

The Library includes extensive free materials about personal, professional and organization development. The Library includes over 675 topics that are organized into the following popular categories. The list of topics is located at http://www.managementhelp.org/ on the Web.

Advertising and Promotion	Benefits and Compensation	Boards of Directors
Career Development	Chief Executive Role	Communications (Interprsnl)
Communications (Writing)	Computers, Internet & Web	Consultants (using)
Coordinating Activities	Creativity and Innovation	Crisis Management
Customer Satisfaction	Customer Service	E-Commerce
Employee Performance	Employee Wellness Programs	Ethics - Practical Toolkit
Evaluations (many kinds)	Facilities Management	Finances (For-Profit)
Finances (Nonprofit)	Fundraising (Nonprofit)	General Resources
Group Performance	Group Skills	Guiding Skills
Human Resources Mgmnt	Insurance (Business)	Interpersonal Skills
Interviewing (all kinds)	Jobs	Leadership (Introduction)
Leadership Development	Legal Information	Management (Introduction)
Management Development	Marketing	Operations Management
Organizational Alliances	Organizational Change	Org'l Communications
Organizational Performance	Organizations (Introduction)	Organizing (many kinds)
Performance Management	Personal Development	Personal Productivity
Personal Wellness	Planning (many kinds)	Policies (Personnel)
Product Selection & Dev.	Program Management	Project Management
Public and Media Relations	Quality Management	Research Methods
Risk Management	Sales	Social Entrepreneurship
Staffing	Starting an Organization	Supervision (Introduction)
Supervisory Development	Systems Thinking	Taxation
Training Basics	Volunteers	----------------

Free Nonprofit Micro-eMBA^{SM} Organization Development Program

This state-of-the-art, on-line training program includes 12 highly integrated courses that can be taken free by anyone, anywhere at any time. At the end of the program, each learner will have all of the basic systems and processes needed to start and operate a nonprofit. Learners are encouraged to work with their Boards of Directors while going through the program. Members share plans, policies and procedures.

Any of the 12 courses in the program can be taken separately. Your organization may also have a wide range of materials around which you could organize courses. To see the courses and their learning objectives, go to the "Course Catalog" located at http://www.managementhelp.org/np_progs/org_dev.htm on the World Wide Web.

Courses include the following

1. Preparatory Workshop (skills in reading, studying, getting help, etc.)

2. Starting and Understanding Your Nonprofit

3. Overview of Role of Chief Executive

4. Basic Skills in Management and Leadership

5. Building and Maintaining an Effective Board of Directors

6. Developing Your Strategic Plan

7. Designing and Marketing Your Programs

8. Managing Your Finances and Taxes

9. Developing Your Fundraising Plan

10. Staffing and Supervision of Employees and Volunteers

11. Evaluating Your Programs

12. Organizational "Fitness Test"

Organizations Assisting Nonprofits

In the USA:

1.   Contact your Secretary of State and/or state's Attorney General's office and ask for a list of resources.

2.   Executive Service Corps (ESC) provides experienced consultation in the areas of technical and managerial services (http://www.escus.org/flash/where-we-serve.html).

3.   National Council of Nonprofit Associations (NCNA) has chapters in almost all of the states (http://www.ncna.org/index.cfm?fuseaction=Page.viewPage&pageId=342).

In Canada:

1.   The Voluntary Sector Knowledge Network provides information, assistance and tools regarding a wide range of functions in nonprofits (http://www.vskn.ca/).

2.   United Way Canada provides information, publications and funding to Canada voluntary sector organizations (http://www.unitedway.ca/english/).

3.   The Canadian Centre for Philanthropy provides programs, resources, tools and information for the benefit of Canadian communities (http://www.ccp.ca/).

General Resources:

1.   Contact the local volunteer recruitment organization in your community and ask for assistance.

2.   Look in the Yellow Pages of your local telephone directory for professional associations. Look for networks or associations of organization development practitioners, facilitators or trainers.

3.   Look in the Yellow Pages of your local telephone directory under the categories "Consultant" and "Volunteering".

4.   Contact local large corporations. They often have community service programs and can provide a wide range of management and technical expertise. Speak to the head of the Human Resources Department.

5.   Call a local university or college and speak to someone in the college of Human Resources, Training and Development, or Business Administration.

6.   Ask other nonprofits (particularly those that have similar services and number of staff,) or current clients for ideas, contacts and references.

7.   Ask a retired business person (from a for-profit or nonprofit organization). Often, they have facilitated a wide variety of meetings.

Free, On-Line Newsletters and Forums

1. **CharityChannel forums**
    CharityChannel provides a wide array of forums, including forums on Canada-specific topics. Go to http://www.charitychannel.com/ on the Web.

2. **PULSE**
    on-line newsletter published by the Support Centers of America and the Nonprofit Management Association. To subscribe, send an e-mail message to "sca@supportcenter.org" and, in the body of the message, type "SUBSCRIBE PULSE!". Or, call (415) 541-7708.

3. **Board Cafe**
    is a free on-line newsletter for nonprofit Boards of Directors, edited by Jan Masaoka, The Chief Executive of the Support Center for Nonprofit Management (an affiliate of the Support Centers of America). To subscribe, send an e-mail message to "msimpson@supportcenter.org" and in the body of the message, type "SUBSCRIBE BOARD CAFE". Or, call (415)-541-9000.

Additional newsletters and forums are listed in the Free Management Library under the topic "General Resources."

Appendix C:
Checklist of Nonprofit Management Indicators

Note that the following checklist, or assessment tool, originally developed by the Greater Twin Cities United Way of Minnesota (USA), has been slightly modified by the author to make it relevant to nonprofit organizations in Canada, as well as the United States. This checklist is used here with the permission of the Greater Twin Cities United Way.

Description

The following checklist is a resource developed by staff and volunteers of the Greater Twin Cities United Way for internal use by nonprofit organizations. Management can use the checklist to identify their organization's administrative strengths and weaknesses. It is believed that widespread use of the checklist ultimately results in a more effective and efficient nonprofit community. The checklist is not intended to be used as a tool for external evaluation, or by grant makers in making funding decisions. This tool will be used to assist nonprofit organizations to gain a better understanding of their management needs and/or make improvements to management operations.

This checklist includes the following topics:

- How to Use the Tool

- Disclaimers

- Legal Indicators

- Governance (Board) Indicators

- Human Resources Indicators

- Planning Indicators

- Financial Indicators

- Fundraising Indicators

How to Use the Tool

Five of the above-listed topics include a variety of indicators for that topic. Each of the many indicators in this tool suggests a management practice needed to have a healthy, well-managed organization. Since it is a self-assessment tool, organizations should evaluate themselves honestly against each indicator and use the response to change or strengthen its operations.

Ratings of Each Indicator

Each indicator is rated based on its importance to the operation and effectiveness of the organization. Thus, the ratings could be interpreted as representing "best practices." The ratings are:

1.   **E** – Indicators marked with an "E" are essential or basic requirements to the operations of all organizations. Organizations that do not meet the terms of these indicators could be placing their organizations in jeopardy.

2.   **R** – Indicators marked with an "R" are recommended as standard practices for effective organizations.

3.   **A** – Indicators marked with an "A" can enhance and strengthen operations.

Possible Responses to Each Indicator

Organizations can respond in one of three ways to each indicator used:

1.   **Met** – Each indicator marked as "Met" indicates that the organization has met the terms of that indicator. However, the organization should review this indicator again in the future to be sure that their management remains healthy in view of the many internal and external changes, which constantly occur in all organizations.

2.   **Needs work** – Each indicator marked as "Needs Work" indicates that work is yet to be done towards meeting the terms of that indicator. The organization is aware of the terms for that indicator, and is working towards meeting those terms.

3.   **N/A** – An indicator marked as "N/A" can indicate several conditions, including:
       - the indicator is not applicable to the management operations of this organization.
       - the organization is not sure of the need to meet the requirements of this indicator.
       - the organization has not met, nor is working on this indicator presently, but may
          address it in the future.

Analysis of Responses to Indicators

All responses to indicators should be reviewed carefully to see if they could improve management operations. Indicators checked "N/A" due to uncertain applicability to the organization must be further reviewed to determine if they should become a part of "doing business." If the assessors simply do not know what the indicator means, further information may be needed to accurately assess the feasibility of its application. Indicators marked "N/A" because they have not been met but that apply to the organization, may require immediate attention. Technical assistance, consulting or training may be required to implement these indicators.

The indicators in this checklist should be informative and thought provoking. The checklist can be used to achieve not only a beginning level of good management, but improve existing management to provide the organization with greater stability, reliability and success. It is particularly useful if an organization is experiencing management problems, to help pinpoint any weaknesses so action can be taken or assistance sought to improve the organization's health. All organizations should use the checklist to re-assess themselves periodically to ensure compliance with established rules and regulations, and to continue improving administrative health through the indicator's helpful suggestions.

Disclaimer

As advised throughout this Field Guide, you should be careful when selecting and applying assessment tools so as not to convey that the tool is somehow a pre-determined, standard "solution" to your client's issues. Information gleaned from assessments should be informed by your knowledge of organizations and causes of issues in them. The assessment tools should be selected in collaboration with your client and according to the nature and needs of your client's organization.

This checklist is designed to provide accurate and authoritative information regarding the topics covered. Legal requirements and non-legal administrative practice standards reflected herein are susceptible to change due to new legislation, regulatory and judicial pronouncements, and updated and evolving guidelines. The checklist may be utilized only with the understanding that the provision of this checklist does not constitute the rendering of legal, tax or other professional services.

If the organization requires professional assistance on these or other legal, governance or management issues, please contact your own professional advisors.

Legal Activities

Rating *	Indicator	Met	Needs Work	N/A
E	1. All relevant legal filings are current and have been made according to the laws and regulations of the nonprofit's country. (For example, in the USA, requirements might include: Annual Registration, Articles of Incorporation with all amendments, Change of Corporate Name, Change of Corporate Address.)			
E	2. The organization is registered with and has filed its annual report with the appropriate governmental agency. (For example, in the USA, the report might be filed with the state's Attorney General's office.)			
E	3. For organizations operating on a tax-exempt basis, the organization has filed the necessary government form to obtain tax-exempt status. (For example, in the USA, the IRS form 1023 was filed and the IRS provided a letter of determination. If the Form 1023 was either filed after 7/15/87 or was in the organization's possession on this date, it is made available for public inspection.)			
E	4. Tax reports are filed on a regular basis. (For example, for tax-exempt organizations in the USA, the IRS form 990 and 990T for unrelated business income, if required, have been filed and copies of the 990 are available to the public.)			
E	5. Federal and state (or provincial) payroll tax withholding payments are current. (This requirement applies to organizations with employees.)			
E	6. Quarterly and annual payroll report filings are current. (This requirement applies to organizations with employees.)			
E	7. If the organization has qualified employee health and/or welfare and/or retirement benefit plans, they meet with all the federal and state/provincial laws. (For example, in the USA, COBRA; initial IRS registration; plan documents; annual filings of the 5500 C/R with copies available to employees.) This requirement applies to organizations with employees.			
E	8. Organization acknowledges and discloses to their Board and auditor any lawsuits or pending legislation which may have a significant impact on the organization's finances and/or operating effectiveness.			
E	9. When the Board of Directors makes decisions, a quorum is present and minutes are maintained.			
E	10. If the organization is subject to sales tax, federal, state/provincial and/or city, filings and payments are current.			
E	11. Organizations that participate in grassroots or direct lobbying have complied with all necessary filings and government regulations.			
E	12. Organizations that conduct charitable gambling have complied with government regulations.			
E	13. Organizations with employees represented by a union must have copies of the union contracts on file.			
E	14. Organizations that operate in a fiscal or host-organization relationship with another organization or group have a written agreement on file.			
Indicators ratings: E=essential; R=recommended; A=additional to strengthen organizational activities				

Governance

Rating *	Indicator	Met	Needs Work	N/A
E	1. The roles of the Board and the Chief Executive Officer are defined and respected, with the Chief Executive Officer delegated as the manager of the organization's operations and the Board focused on policy and planning.			
R	2. The Chief Executive Officer is recruited, selected and employed by the Board of Directors. The Board provides clearly written expectations and qualifications for the position, as well as reasonable compensation.			
R	3. The Board of Directors acts as governing trustees of the organization on behalf of the community at large and contributors, while carrying out the organization's mission and goals. To fully meet this goal, the Board of Directors must actively participate in the planning process (as outlined in planning sections of this checklist).			
R	4. The Board's nominating process ensures that the Board remains appropriately diverse with respect to gender, ethnicity, culture, economic status, disabilities, and skills and/or expertise.			
E	5. The Board members receive regular training and information about their responsibilities.			
E	6. New Board members are oriented to the organization, including the organization's mission, bylaws, policies and programs, as well as their roles and responsibilities as Board members.			
A	7. Board organization is documented with a description of the Board and Board committee responsibilities.			
A	8. Each Board member has, and is familiar with, the Board operations manual.			
E	9. If the organization has any related party transactions between Board members or their families, they are disclosed to the Board of Directors (in the USA, the Internal Revenue Service and the auditor).			
E	10. The organization has at least the minimum number of members on the Board of Directors as required by their bylaws or federal and state/provincial statute.			
R	11. If the organization has adopted bylaws, they conform to state/provincial statutes and have been reviewed by legal counsel.			
R	12. The bylaws should include, at a minimum: a) how and when notices for Board meetings are made; b) how members are elected/appointed by the Board; c) what the terms of office are for officers/members; d) how Board members are rotated; e) how ineffective Board members are removed from the Board; and f) a stated number of Board members to make up a quorum which is required for all policy decisions.			
R	13. The Board of Directors reviews the bylaws at least yearly.			
A	14. The Board has a process for handling urgent matters between meetings.			
E	15. Board members serve without payment unless the agency has a policy identifying reimbursable out-of-pocket expenses.			
R	16. The organization maintains a conflict-of-interest and Board attendance policy and all Board members and executive staff review and sign the policies to acknowledge compliance with the policies.			
R	17. The Board has and implements an annual calendar of Board activities. The Board also achieves at least a quorum of Board members in each meeting.			

Used with permission of Greater Twin Cities United Way.

Governance (Cont.)

Rating *	Indicator	Met	Needs Work	N/A
A	18. Meetings have written agendas, and materials relating to significant decisions are given to the Board in advance of the meeting.			
A	19. The Board has a written policy prohibiting employees and members of employees' immediate families from serving as Board Chair or Treasurer.			
Indicators ratings: E=essential; R=recommended; A=additional to strengthen organizational activities				

Human Resources – Staff and Volunteers

Staff

Rating *	Indicator	Met	Needs Work	N/A
E	1. The organization has a written personnel handbook/policy that is regularly reviewed and updated, and at a minimum: a) describes the recruitment, hiring, termination and standard work rules for all staff; b) and maintains compliance with government employment laws and regulations. (For example, in the USA, this includes Fair Labor Standards Act, Equal Employment Opportunity Act, Americans with Disabilities Act, Occupational Health and Safety Act, Family Leave Act, Affirmative Action Plan if required, etc.)			
R	2. The organization follows nondiscriminatory hiring practices.			
R	3. The organization provides a copy of or access to the written personnel policy to all members of the Board, the Chief Executive Officer and all staff members. All staff members acknowledge in writing that they have read and understand the personnel handbook/policies.			
R	4. The organization has job descriptions including qualifications, duties, reporting relationships and key indicators of performance.			
R	5. The organization's Board of Directors conducts an annual review/evaluation of its Chief Executive Officer in relationship to a previously determined set of performance expectations.			
R	6. The Chief Executive Officer's salary is set by the Board of Directors in a reasonable process and is in compliance with the organization's compensation plan.			
R	7. The organization requires employee performance appraisals to be conducted and documented at least annually.			
A	8. The organization has a compensation plan, and a periodic review of salary ranges and benefits is conducted.			
A	9. The organization has a timely process for filling vacant positions to prevent an interruption of program services or disruption to organization operations.			
A	10. The organization has a process for reviewing and responding to ideas, suggestions, comments and perceptions from all staff members.			
A	11. The organization provides opportunities for employees' professional development and training within their job skill area and also in such areas as cultural sensitivity and personal development.			
A	12. The organization maintains contemporaneous records documenting staff time in program allocations.			
Indicators ratings: E=essential; R=recommended; A=additional to strengthen organizational activities				

Human Resources – Staff and Volunteers (Cont.)

Volunteers

Rating *	Indicator	Met	Needs Work	N/A
E	13. The organization has clearly defined the roles that volunteers have within the organization.			
E	14. Job descriptions exist for all volunteer positions in the organization.			
R	15. The organization has a well-defined and communicated volunteer management plan that includes, at a minimum: a) a recruitment policy, b) a description of all volunteer jobs, c) an application and interview process, d) possible stipend and reimbursement policies, e) a statement of which staff has supervisory responsibilities over what volunteers, and f) any other volunteer personnel policy information.			
E	16. The organization follows a recruitment policy that does not discriminate, but respects, encourages and represents the diversity of the community.			
E	17. The organization provides appropriate training and orientation to assist the volunteer in the performance of their activities. Volunteers are offered training with staff in, for example, cultural sensitivity.			
E	18. The organization ensures background checks and liability insurance to ensure low-risk utilization of volunteers' skills.			
R	19. The organization is respectful of the volunteer's abilities and time commitment and has various job duties to meet these needs. Jobs should not be given to volunteers simply because the jobs are considered inferior for paid staff.			
R	20. The organization does volunteer performance appraisals periodically and communicates to the volunteers how well they are doing, or where additional attention is needed. At the same time, volunteers are requested to review and evaluate their involvement in the organization and the people they work with and suggest areas for improvement.			
R	21. The organization does some type of volunteer recognition or commendation periodically and staff continuously demonstrates their appreciation towards the volunteers and their efforts.			
A	22. The organization has a process for reviewing and responding to ideas, suggestions, comments and perceptions from volunteers.			
A	23. The organization provides opportunities for program participants to volunteer.			
A	24. The organization maintains contemporaneous records documenting volunteer time in program allocations. Financial records can be maintained for the volunteer time spent on programs and recorded as in-kind contributions.			
Indicators ratings: E=essential; R=recommended; A=additional to strengthen organizational activities				

Planning (Strategic and Programs)

Strategic Planning

Rating *	Indicator	Met	Needs Work	N/A
E	1. The organization's purpose and activities meet community needs.			
R	2. The organization frequently evaluates, by soliciting community input, whether its mission and activities provide benefit to the community.			
R	3. The organization has a values statement that is reflected in the agency's activities and is communicated by its constituents.			
A	4. The values statement includes standards of ethical behavior and respect for other's interests.			
E	5. The organization has a clear, meaningful written mission statement which reflects its purpose, values and people served.			
R	6. The Board and staff periodically review the mission statement and modify it to reflect changes in the environment.			
E	7. The Board and staff develop and adopt a written Strategic Plan to achieve its mission.			
A	8. Board, staff, service recipients, volunteers, key constituents and general members of the community participate in the planning process.			
E	9. The plan was developed after researching the internal and external environments.			
R	10. The plan identifies changing community needs.			
R	11. The planning process identifies the critical issues facing the organization (including the agency's strengths, weaknesses, opportunities and threats).			
R	12. The plan sets goals and measurable objectives that address these critical issues.			
E	13. The plan integrates all the organization's activities around a focused mission.			
R	14. The plan prioritizes the agency goals and develops timelines for their accomplishment.			
A	15. The plan establishes an evaluation process and performance indicators to measure the progress toward the achievement of goals and objectives.			
R	16. Through work plans, human and financial resources are allocated to ensure the accomplishment of the goals in a timely fashion.			
A	17. The plan is communicated to all stakeholders of the agency – service recipients, Board, staff, volunteers and the general community.			
Indicators ratings: E=essential; R=recommended; A=additional to strengthen organizational activities				

Planning (Cont.)

Planning Regarding the Organization's Programs

Rating *	Indicator	Met	Needs Work	N/A
E	1. Programs are congruent with the agency's mission and Strategic Plan.			
A	2. The organization actively informs the public about its programs and services.			
A	3. Clients and potential clients have the opportunity to participate in program development.			
R	4. Sufficient resources are allocated to ensure each program can achieve the established goals and objectives for each program.			
R	5. Staff has sufficient training and skill level to produce the program.			
A	6. Programs within the organization are integrated to provide more complete services to clients.			
R	7. Each program has performance indicators to insure that attainment or goals can be measured.			
R	8. Performance indicators are reviewed annually.			
A	9. The agency networks and/or collaborates with other organizations to produce the most comprehensive and effective services to clients.			
Indicators ratings: E=essential; R=recommended; A=additional to strengthen organizational activities				

Planning Regarding the Organization's Evaluations

Rating *	Indicator	Met	Needs Work	N/A
R	1. Every year, the organization evaluates its activities to determine progress toward goal accomplishment.			
A	2. Stakeholders are involved in the evaluation process.			
R	3. The evaluation includes a review of organizational programs and systems to insure that they comply with the organization's mission, values and goals.			
R	4. The results of the evaluation are reflected in the revised plan.			
A	5. Periodically, the organization conducts a comprehensive evaluation of its programs. This evaluation measures program outcomes.			
Indicators ratings: E=essential; R=recommended; A=additional to strengthen organizational activities				

Financial Activities

Rating *	Indicator	Met	Needs Work	N/A
E	1. The organization follows accounting practices which conform to generally accepted accounting standards.			
E	2. The organization has systems in place to provide the appropriate information needed by staff and Board to make sound financial decisions and to fulfill government requirements (for example, in the USA, the Internal Revenue Service).			
R	3. The organization prepares timely financial statements including the balance sheet, income statement and cash flow statement which are clearly stated and useful for the Board and staff. (Note that these statements might be referred to by different names in various countries.)			
R	4. The organization prepares financial statements on a budget-versus-actual and/or comparative basis to achieve a better understanding of their finances.			
E	5. The organization develops an annual comprehensive operating budget which includes costs for all programs, management and fundraising and all sources of funding. This budget is reviewed and approved by the Board of Directors.			
R	6. The organization monitors unit costs of programs and services through the documentation of staff time and direct expenses and use of a process for allocation of management, general and fundraising expenses.			
E	7. The organization prepares cash flow projections.			
R	8. The organization periodically forecasts year-end revenues and expenses to assist in making sound management decisions during the year.			
E	9. The organization reconciles all cash accounts monthly.			
E	10. The organization has a review process to monitor that they are receiving appropriate and accurate financial information whether from a contracted service or internal processing.			
E	11. If the organization has billable contracts or other service income, procedures are established for the periodic billing, follow-up and collection of all accounts, and the documentation that substantiates all billings.			
E	12. Government contracts, purchase of service agreements and grant agreements are in writing and are reviewed by a staff member of the organization to monitor compliance with all stated conditions.			
E	13. Payroll is prepared following appropriate federal and state/provincial regulations and organizational policy.			
E	14. Persons employed on a contract basis meet all federal and state/provincial requirements for this form of employment. (In the USA, disbursement records are kept so 1099's can be issued at year end.)			
E	15. Organizations that purchase and sell merchandise take periodic inventories to monitor the inventory against theft, to reconcile general ledger inventory information and to maintain an adequate inventory level.			
R	16. The organization has a written fiscal policy and procedures manual and follows it.			
E	17. The organization has documented a set of internal controls, including handling of cash and deposits, statement reconciliation, approval over spending and disbursements.			

Financial Activities (Cont.)

Rating *	Indicator	Met	Needs Work	N/A
E	18. The organization has a policy identifying authorized check signers and the number of signatures required on checks in excess of specified dollar amounts.			
E	19. All expenses of the organization are approved by a designated person before payment is made.			
R	20. The organization has a written policy related to investments.			
R	21. Capital needs are reviewed at least annually and priorities established.			
R	22. The organization has established a plan identifying actions to take in the event of a reduction or loss in funding.			
R	23. The organization has established, or is actively trying to develop, a reserve of funds to cover at least three months of operating expenses.			
E	24. The organization has suitable insurance coverage which is periodically reviewed to ensure the appropriate levels and types of coverage are in place.			
E	25. Employees, Board members and volunteers who handle cash and investments are bonded to help assure the safeguarding of assets.			
E	26. The organization files forms in regard to tax-exempt and/or tax-deductible (charity) status on a timely basis.			
R	27. The organization reviews income annually to determine and report unrelated business income to the necessary government agency (for example, to the IRS in the USA).			
R	28. The organization has an annual, independent audit of their financial statements, prepared by a certified public accountant.			
R	29. In addition to the audit, the auditor prepares a management letter containing recommendations for improvements in the financial operations of the organization.			
R	30. The Board of Directors, or an appropriate committee, is responsible for soliciting bids, interviewing auditors and hiring an auditor for the organization.			
E	31. The Board of Directors, or an appropriate committee, reviews and approves the audit report and management letter and with staff input and support, institutes any necessary changes.			
E	32. The audit, or an organization-prepared annual report which includes financial statements, is made available to service recipients, volunteers, contributors, funders and other interested parties.			
A	33. Training is made available for Board and appropriate staff on relevant accounting topics and all appropriate persons are encouraged to participate in various training opportunities.			
Indicators ratings: E=essential; R=recommended; A=additional to strengthen organizational activities				

Fundraising Activities

General Fundraising

Rating *	Indicator	Met	Needs Work	N/A
E	1. Funds are raised in an ethical manner for activities consistent with the organization's mission and plans.			
E	2. The Board of Directors and organization staff are knowledgeable about the fundraising process and the roles in the organization.			
E	3. The organization's Board of Directors has established a committee charged with developing, evaluating and reviewing fundraising policies, practices and goals.			
E	4. The committee is actively involved in the fundraising process and works to involve others in these activities.			
R	5. The Board of Directors, Chief Executive Officer and committee supports and participates in the total fundraising process, including project identification, cultivation, solicitation and recognition. Each Board member contributes financially and/or in-kind to the organization.			
R	6. The fundraising program is staffed and funded at a level consistent with fundraising expectations.			
A	7. There is direct communication and relationship between information services and marketing to assist in the fundraising needs and efforts.			
E	8. The organization is accountable to donors and other key constituencies and demonstrates their stewardship through annual reports.			
Indicators ratings: E=essential; R=recommended; A=additional to strengthen organizational activities				

Fundraising (Cont.)

Using an Outside Fundraiser

Rating *	Indicator	Met	Needs Work	N/A
A	9. The organization meets the nonprofit standards of the state/provincial charities review council, if one exists.			
R	10. If the organization chooses to use outside professional fundraisers, several competitive bids are solicited. Each prospective outside fundraiser's background and references are checked.			
E	11. The organization makes legal, mutually agreed upon, signed statements with outside professional fundraisers, outlining each parties' responsibilities and duties, specifying how the contributed funds will be physically handled, and guaranteeing that the fees to be paid are reasonable and fair.			
E	12. The organization has verified that the contracted fundraiser is registered as a professional fundraiser with the appropriate government agency and all filings necessary have been made before the work commences.			
E	13. The fundraising committee or appropriate representatives from the Board of Directors reviews all prospective proposals with the outside professional fundraiser and reviews and accepts all agreements before they are signed.			
R	14. If the outside professional fundraiser plans to contact potential donors directly, the organization reviews the fundraising materials (e.g., public service announcements, print or broadcast advertisements, telemarketing scripts, pledge statements, brochures, letters, etc.) to verify their accuracy and to ensure that the public disclosure requirements have been met.			
E	15. The organization properly reports all required information regarding use of outside professional fundraisers, amount of funds raised and the related fundraising expenses as required by federal and state/provincial governments. The gross amount of funds raised by the contracted fundraiser is reported on the organization's financial statement. The fees and costs of the campaign must be reported on the statement of functional expenses.			
Indicators ratings: E=essential; R=recommended; A=additional to strengthen organizational activities				

Appendix D: Worksheets

The publisher of this Field Guide gives permission to the owner of this Field Guide to duplicate these worksheets within their organization, preserving our copyright notice at the bottom of each worksheet. Consultants may duplicate worksheets to use with their clients as long as each client organization owns at least one copy of the Field Guide. Note that these worksheets are also available on-line at http://www.authenticityconsulting.com/pubs/PG_gdes/worksheets.doc
NOTE: It might take a couple of minutes to download this file.

The worksheets are ordered and grouped below according to the sections of this Field Guide.

Developing Program Layout and Logic Model

1. Assessment of Community Needs and Interests

2. Vision for Program Participants

3. Desired Outcomes for Program Participants

4. Methods to Help Participants Achieve Desired Outcomes

5. Outcomes Goals/Targets and Indicators toward Hitting Targets

6. Outputs/Tangibles Produced by Methods

7. Preliminary Program Logic Model

Marketing Analysis

1. Target Markets, Their Features and Benefits They Perceive

2. Packaging Analysis

3. Unique Value Proposition Description

4. Program Name Analysis

5. Pricing Analysis

6. Competitor Analysis

7. Collaborator Analysis

8. Laws and Regulations

9. Description of Service

10. Summary of Remaining Market Analysis Tasks and Considerations

11. Marketing Goals

Planning Program Development

1.   Planning Program Development (One-Time, Start-Up Activities)

Planning Program Operations

1.   Advertising and Promotions

2.   Sales Planning

3.   Customer Service Planning

4.   Delivery of Services

5.   Personnel Needs

6.   Materials (Supplies, Tools, Equipment and Facilities)

Financial Planning

1.   Program Budget

Evaluation Planning

1.   Planning Your Program Evaluation

The section, "Developing Program Framework," includes guidelines to help you complete this worksheet.

Assessment of Community Needs and Interests

What were the various community needs that you identified during your needs assessment?

What is your ranking of the various community needs in terms of those you most prefer to meet with a program?

What is the overall, top-ranked major community need that your program intends to meet?
Write your description in terms of their need, not yours.

Assessment of Community Needs and Interests (Cont.)

Is the need urgent or important? How did you come to that conclusion?

Describe what you believe are the causes of the need, that is, how did it come about?

What research have you conducted to verify the existence, and your understanding, of this overall, top-ranked need in your community?

Assessment of Community Needs and Interests (Cont.)

What specific community groups have the need? You might differentiate groups by considering common preferences, ages, locations, experiences, etc.

What are your preliminary thoughts about how the need might be met? You will likely refine your description when completing additional worksheets.

Are there any remaining activities that you believe should be carried out to fully conduct your needs assessment?

The section, "Developing Program Framework," includes guidelines to help you complete this worksheet.

Vision for Program Participants

Collect your thoughts about your vision for the community (or client) groups. What would various groups of clients look like, or be doing, after they have met their needs from participating in your program?

Now, in your own writing style, write a powerful, yet concise description of your vision. Be as specific as possible, including the types of various community groups served by your programs, and successes they will achieve from participating in your program.

Vision for Program Participants (Cont.)

How does the vision directly relate to the problem or need that you have identified?

Is this vision realistic? Why is it realistic? Why is not it realistic?

Is the vision closely related to your mission? Should your mission be modified and, if so, how?

Are there any remaining activities that you believe should be carried out to establish description of a clear, realistic, useful vision?

The section, "Developing Program Framework," includes guidelines to help you complete this worksheet.

Desired Outcomes for Program Participants

What outcomes do clients need to achieve to have their needs met? Consider:

Changed knowledge?

Changed behaviors?

Changed attitudes, values, conditions, status, etc.?

Desired Outcomes for Program Participants (Cont.)

If you have identified several outcomes, consider which are the most important outcomes to achieve and in what order?

From those most important outcomes, attempt to identify short-term, intermediate and long-term outcomes.

Short-term Outcomes (three to six months after program)

Intermediate Outcomes (six to 12 months after program)

Long-Term Outcomes (12-24 months after program)

Are there any remaining activities that you believe should be carried out to identify the most relevant, realistic and important outcomes to pursue?

The section, "Developing Program Framework," includes guidelines to help you complete this worksheet.

Methods to Help Participants Achieve Desired Outcomes

What methods are you seeing or hearing that might work to help participants to achieve the desired outcomes? Consider:

- What are other similar nonprofits doing to achieve their outcomes?

- What have clients said that needs to be done to meet their needs?

- What do your staff members say that needs to be done?

- Any advice from experts in the field?

- Related studies or research efforts?

- Any advice from funders?

What additional or other methods should your program implement?

Methods to Help Participants Achieve Desired Outcomes (Cont.)

How are these methods realistic for your program to pursue?

How are these methods closely related to your mission?

What research did you do to select the methods?

What research do you have yet to do to verify the best methods?

Are there any remaining activities that you believe should be carried out to identify the most relevant, mission-related and realistic methods?

Outcomes Goals/Targets and Indicators toward Hitting Targets

The section, "Developing Program Framework," includes guidelines to help you complete this worksheet.

Outcome	Outcome Goal / Target	Indicator(s)
Most important outcomes, or changes, for program to help participants achieve.	Number and/or percent of participants to achieve outcome during time period. One goal/target per outcome.	Observable and measurable "milestones" toward achieving each outcome target. Usually requires several indicators per outcome goal/target.
	Realistic?	
	Realistic?	
	Realistic?	

Any remaining activities that you believe should be carried out to identify outcome targets and indicators?

Preliminary Program Logic Model

The section, "Developing Program Framework," includes guidelines to help you complete this worksheet.

Inputs	Processes	Outputs	Short-Term Outcomes	Intermediate Outcomes	Long-Term Outcomes

Any remaining activities that you believe should be carried out to complete the logic model?

Target Markets, Their Features and Benefits They Perceive

The section, "Marketing Analysis," includes guidelines to help you complete this worksheet.

Target Markets	Their Common Features (For example, common location, interests, experiences, status, etc.)	Benefits They Might Perceive in Program (For example, easy access, affordable, complementary services, affiliation, etc.)
Target Market # 1		
Target Market # 2		
Target Market # 3		

How did you research the target markets, their features and perceived program benefits? Any remaining research to do?

The section, "Marketing Analysis," includes guidelines to help you complete this worksheet.

Packaging Analysis

Describe how to package the services to best accommodate the needs of each target market. Consider:

- How they access the service, for example, should clients come to your facility, will you visit their offices, or can you provide services over the telephone or Internet?

- Their capabilities to understand the program and how to use it

- Options for scheduling

- Options for the amount of attention to them

- Others?

How did you select the best packaging combinations?

Any additional activities that you believe should be carried out to complete your packaging analysis for your service to your target market?

The section, "Marketing Analysis," includes guidelines to help you complete this worksheet.

Unique Value Proposition Description

For each target market, describe the benefits of the program. Consider:

- Low pricing
- High quality
- Good atmosphere
- Great location
- Easier access to services
- Great customer service
- Others?

Who did you include in the review of your proposition? What did they think of it?

Any additional activities that you believe should be carried out to complete the unique value proposition for your service to your target market?

The section, "Marketing Analysis," includes guidelines to help you complete this worksheet. Be sure to copy and complete this worksheet for each preferred name.

Program Name Analysis

How does the name accurately portray the nature of the service(s) offered by your program?

What do others think of the name?

Have you verified that no other similar organizations use a similar name by
(For example in the USA):

☐ Looking in the Yellow Pages of your local telephone directory

☐ Calling the local chapter of the National Council of Nonprofit Associations

☐ Calling the Secretary of State's office to see if similar names are registered

☐ Looking in federal database at the Patents and Trademark Offices at http://www.uspto.gov/

How will the name fit as your program continues to grow?

Any additional activities that you believe should be carried out to complete your naming analysis for your service to your target market?

The section, "Marketing Analysis," includes guidelines to help you complete this worksheet. Answers to some of these questions can be refined later, during operations planning.

Pricing Analysis

How much will it cost you to provide the service? Estimate time, people and materials costs.

How will you recover your costs to produce and provide the service?

What fee would be affordable to clients?

How do you know that fee would be affordable?

How would that fee be competitive? Consider what competitors are charging.

Pricing Analysis (Cont.)

How do you know that fee would be competitive?

What pricing structure should you use for this service (for example, sliding-fee scale, deferred payments, installment payments, etc.)?

How do you know what pricing structure should be used?

What warranty or service policies should you have in place?

What return or exchange policy should you have in place?

What credit terms should you offer? What will they cost?

Any additional activities that you believe should be carried out to complete your pricing analysis for your service to your target market?

The section, "Marketing Analysis," includes guidelines to help you complete this worksheet. Be sure to copy and complete this worksheet for each competitor.

Competitor Analysis

Name of competitor's organization

Describe their service(s) that compete with yours.

Describe the common target market.

What are the benefits of their service(s) to the target market?

Compare their pricing and yours.

How do they advertise their services? What messages do they convey in their advertising and promotions?

Competitor Analysis (Cont.)

How do they package and provide their services?

What are the strengths and weaknesses of their services?

How does your overall services(s) compare to theirs?

How will you compete? Lower prices? More convenient location? Better service?

Any additional activities that need to be carried out to complete the competitive analysis for your service to this target market?

The section, "Marketing Analysis," includes guidelines to help you complete this worksheet. Be sure to copy and complete this worksheet for each collaborator.

Collaborator Analysis

Name of potential collaborator's organization

Name of their service

Compare and contrast your services and theirs.

What are potential areas of collaboration?

What are the advantages of collaboration?

What are potential disadvantages of collaboration?

Any additional activities that you believe should be carried out to complete your collaborator analysis for your service to your target market?

The section, "Marketing Analysis," includes guidelines to help you complete this worksheet. Be sure to copy and complete this worksheet for *each* target market that might have unique regulations, whether by geography (local government) or field (health and social services).

Laws and Regulations

What kinds of taxes might you have to pay? In the USA, will you need a Federal Employer Identification Number?

What kinds of insurance might you need/prefer?

☐	Automobile	☐	Business Interruption
☐	Property damage	☐	Key Person
☐	General liability	☐	Health or Medical
☐	Product liability	☐	Directors and Officers
☐	Disability	☐	Others
☐	Workers Compensation		

What licenses or permits might you need? For example, do you plan to sell products that require a permit to sell?

Laws and Regulations (Cont.)

What kinds of contracts might you need? For example, you might want to hire suppliers and vendors.

What kinds of regulations must you follow if you plan to hire employees? What labor laws are relevant?

What kinds of inspections might you need? Food and health? Buildings? Others?

Any additional activities that you believe should be carried out to complete your identification of relevant laws and regulations for your service?

The section, "Marketing Analysis," includes guidelines to help you complete this worksheet. Be sure to copy and complete this worksheet for each service.

Description of Service

The name of your service is:

The service provides:

You will serve the following markets and provide them with the following benefits:

Target Market	Benefits

Description of Service (Cont.)

The price(s) of your service is:

Clients can pay with the following methods:

The service will be provided in the following forms and formats (packaging):

The section, "Marketing Analysis," includes guidelines to help you complete this worksheet.

Summary of Remaining
Marketing Analysis Tasks and Considerations

Remaining Task or Consideration	Who Is Responsible?	By When?

The section, "Marketing Analysis," includes guidelines to help you complete this worksheet. Be sure the goals are SMART – specific, measurable, achievable, relevant and timely.

Marketing Goals

Goal to Accomplish Over Next Year	Who Is Responsible?	By When?

The section, "Planning Program Development," includes guidelines to help you complete this worksheet.

Program Planning Development

1. How will you design the top-level, conceptual design (logic model) of the program?

What tasks must you complete? This Field Guide includes guidelines to design the logic model. Any other guidelines or tasks needed?

What expertise (people) do you need? Consider who will do the researching, writing and reviewing.

What materials (tools, supplies, equipment, facilities, etc.,) do you need? Where will you get them? What will they cost? Will you have to fix them up?

Any other key considerations in conceptualizing your program?

Program Planning Development (Cont.)

2. How will you conduct a comprehensive marketing analysis?

What tasks must you complete? This Field Guide includes guidelines to conduct the marketing analysis. Any other guidelines or tasks needed?

What expertise (people) do you need? Consider who will do the researching, writing and reviewing.

What materials (tools, supplies, equipment, facilities, etc.,) do you need? Where will you get them? What will they cost? Will you have to fix them up?

Any other key considerations in conducting your market analysis?

Program Planning Development (Cont.)

3. How will you procure and manage the resources required to first build the service?

What tasks must you complete? Consider financial planning, fundraising, purchasing, storage and managing inventory and supplies, etc.

What expertise (people) do you need? Consider roles of program directors or managers, clerical support, Board committees (these are usually volunteers), volunteers to staff, direct-delivery personnel, professionals (accountants, lawyers, fundraisers, etc.). Attempt to identify your needs in terms of full-time-equivalents (FTE's). One FTE is equivalent to one full-time person.

What materials do you need? Consider general office supplies and equipment, tools, general equipment and facilities. Where will you get them? What will they cost? Will you have to fix them up?

Program Planning Development (Cont.)

4. How will you build (and sometimes test) the first version of the service?

What tasks must you complete? Consider developing a prototype, build marketing materials (logos, brochures, web sites, stationery, etc.), testing the prototype with various groups of clients, refining the design of the service, documenting how to provide the service, training others how to use the service, working with various professionals, etc.

What expertise (people) do you need? Consider roles of program directors or managers, clerical support, Board committees (these are usually volunteers), volunteers to staff, direct-delivery personnel, professionals (accountants, lawyers, fundraisers, etc.). Attempt to identify your needs in terms of full-time-equivalents (FTE's). One FTE equals one full-time person.

What materials do you need? Consider general office supplies and equipment, tools, general equipment and facilities. Where will you get them? What will they cost? Will you have to fix them up?

The section, "Planning Program Operations," includes guidelines to help you complete this worksheet. Be sure to copy and complete this worksheet for each target market.

Advertising and Promotions

Target Market:

Primary Messages *What is in it for client?*	Methods to Convey Message (see list below)	When to Use Method

Sources for Advertising
__ Brochures or flyers
__ Direct mail
__ E-mail messages
__ Magazines
__ Newsletters
__ Newspapers (major)
__ Newspapers (neighborhood)
__ On-line discussion groups and chat groups
__ Posters and bulletin boards
__ Radio announcements
__ Telemarketing
__ Television ads

__ Web pages
__ Yellow Pages
__ Other(s)

Promotional Activities through Media
__ Articles that you write
__ Editorials and letters to the editor
__ Press kits
__ Press releases or news alerts
__ Public service announcements (PSAs)
__ Other(s)

Other Promotional Activities and Events
__ Annual reports
__ Collaboration or strategic restructuring
__ Networking
__ Novelties
__ Presentations
__ Relationships with key stakeholders
__ Special events
__ Special offers
__ Other(s)

Any additional activities that you believe should be carried out to complete your advertising and promotions analysis for your service to your target market?

The section, "Planning Program Operations," includes guidelines to help you complete this worksheet. Be sure to copy and complete this worksheet for each target market.

Sales Planning

Target Market:

Methods to generate leads, follow-ups, presentations and closing sales	What materials will you need to support the sales activities? (See Appendix F.)

Any additional activities that you believe should be carried out to complete your sales analysis for your service to your target market?

The section, "Planning Program Operations," includes guidelines to help you complete this worksheet. Be sure to copy and complete this worksheet for each target market.

Customer Service Planning

Target Market:

What policies and procedures are needed to ensure strong customer service?
Consider training, including developing skills in interpersonal relations, questioning, listening, handling difficult people, handling interpersonal conflicts, and negotiating.

How will you detect if customers are satisfied with the service from your program?

How do you know you have chosen the best methods to detect if customers are satisfied?

If they are not satisfied, how will you handle customer complaints?

The section, "Planning Program Operations," includes guidelines to help you complete this worksheet. For each of the following major activities, consider:

- Tasks that need to be done
- Expertise or people needed (roles of program directors or managers, clerical support, Board committees, volunteers to staff, direct-delivery personnel, professionals (accountants, lawyers, fundraisers, etc.)
- Materials needed (tools, supplies, equipment, facilities, etc.)

If you can, think about demand in six months? 12 months?

Delivery of Services

Tasks	Expertise	Materials
Fundraising?		
Purchase supplies and equipment?		

Delivery of Services (Cont.)

Tasks	Expertise	Materials
Office administration (office supplies, property management, clerical support, etc.)?		
Bookkeeping and accounting (information management)?		
Financial analysis (report generation and analysis)?		

Delivery of Services (Cont.)

Tasks	Expertise	Materials
Computer system administration?		
Produce service/product (reproduce resources required for direct delivery of services)?		
Deliver the service to the client (direct contact and service to clients)?		

Delivery of Services (Cont.)

Tasks	Expertise	Materials
Professional services (lawyers, bankers, accountants, etc.)?		
Other(s)?		

Any additional activities that you believe should be carried out to complete the analysis for delivery of your service to your target market?

The section, "Planning Program Operations," includes directions to complete this worksheet. In this section, you pull together all of your human resource needs.

Personnel Needs

Assignments and Human Resource Needs

Ongoing Activities	What Role/Position is Responsible for Activities?	Time Required for Activities (1 "FTE" = full-time)
Fundraising		
Purchase supplies and equipment		
Office administration		
Bookkeeping and accounting		
Financial analysis		
Computer system administration		
Produce service/product		
Advertising and promotion		
Sales and customer service		
Deliver service to clients		
Professional services		
Other(s)?		

Personnel Needs (Cont.)

Organization and Management

Do you have the necessary expertise in-house now or will you have to hire additional help? What additional help might you have to hire?

How will your staff be organized? What roles will report to what other roles? Make sure that each person ultimately reports to one person.

How will your staff be paid? Consider compensation (pay) and benefits.

How will each of your staff members be made clearly aware of his or her responsibilities? Consider updating each member's job description.

Personnel Needs (Cont.)

How will you ensure that staff has sufficient resources to carry out their responsibilities?

How will you ensure that each staff member has adequate supervision, including clear goals, and ongoing delegation and feedback?

What personnel policies will be needed or need to be updated?

What changes are needed to your organization charts?

The section, "Planning Program Operations," includes directions to complete this worksheet. In this section, you pull together all of the materials needed for the ongoing operations. Consider how you will obtain the materials and the costs to obtain and/or fix them up for program use.

Materials
(Supplies, Tools, Equipment and Facilities)

General Equipment and Supplies

General office supplies (paper, pencils, pens, staples, etc.)?

Postage?

Tools?

Computers and peripherals (printers, scanners, etc.)?

Data communications equipment (modems, networking, broadband, etc.)?

Materials (Cont.)

General Equipment and Supplies (Cont.)

Telephones (single-line, multi-line, cell, etc.)?

Copier (black and white, color, stapling, etc.)?

Fax?

Other(s)?

Major Facilities and Equipment

Buildings and physical layout?

Materials (Cont.)

Major Facilities and Equipment (Cont.)

Offices (or office bays) and layout?

Furniture (physical layout)?

Utilities (electricity, water, sewer, heat, etc.)?

Telephone and data communications cabling?

Cleaning services?

Other(s)?

The section, "Planning Finances to Operate Program," includes guidelines to help you complete this worksheet.

Summary Program Budget

Step 1 – Select Time Period for Your Program Budget:

From: To:

Step 2 – Expenses:

Item	Estimated Amount	Commentary
Personnel:	$	
	$	
	$	
	$	
	$	
	$	
	$	
Total Personnel:	$	
Facilities:	$	
	$	
	$	
	$	
	$	
	$	
	$	
Total Facilities:	$	

Summary Program Budget (Cont.)

Other Expenses:	$	
	$	
	$	
	$	
	$	
	$	
	$	
In-kind donations (remember that any in-kind donations must also be expensed)	$	
Total Other Expenses:	$	
Total Expenses:	$	

Step 3 – Revenue:

Earned Income:	$	
Fees from services to clients	$	
Dues from membership	$	
Government contracts	$	
Investment income	$	
	$	
	$	
	$	
	$	
	$	
Total Earned Income:	$	

Summary Program Budget (Cont.)

Contributions:	$	
Grants from foundations	$	
Grants from corporations	$	
Grants from government	$	
Individual contributions	$	
In-kind donations (remember that any in-kind donations must also be expensed)	$	
	$	
	$	
Total Contributions:	$	
Total Revenues:	$	

Step 4 – Balancing Budget:

Total Revenues	
Total Expenses	
Total Revenues Minus Total Expenses	

If the result is less then 0, you have a deficit. If result is greater then 0, you have a surplus.

If you have a deficit, you will:

a) Reduce each of the following expenses by the following amounts:

Expense Items	Amount

Total Expenses Reduction:	

b) And/or increase earned income according to the following terms:

Income Items	Amount
Earned Income:	$
Fees from services to clients	$
Dues from membership	$
Government contracts	$
Investment income	$
Other	$
Total Earned Income Increase:	$

c) And/or increase fundraising expectations by the following amounts:

Fundraising Actions	Amount
Contributions:	$
Grants from foundations	$
Grants from corporations	$
Grants from government	$
Individual contributions	$
Other	$
Total Contributions Increase:	$

The section, "Planning Your Program Evaluation," includes directions to complete these worksheets.

Planning Your Program Evaluation

Name of program to be evaluated:

Audience(s) for the evaluation:

- ☐ Clients/customers
- ☐ Board members
- ☐ Funders/Investors
- ☐ Management
- ☐ Staff/employees
- ☐ Other(s)

Purpose of evaluation (what management decision(s) are needed?):
What do you want to be able to decide as a result of the evaluation? For example:

- ☐ Understand, verify or increase impact of products or services on customers/clients (suggests outcomes evaluation)
- ☐ Improve delivery mechanisms to be more efficient and/or less costly (suggests process evaluation)
- ☐ Verify that you are doing what you think you are doing (could suggest process evaluation)
- ☐ Clarify program goals, processes and outcomes for management planning (could suggest variety of types of evaluations)
- ☐ Public relations (could suggest goals evaluation, if public relations plan and goals had been established)
- ☐ Program comparisons, for example, to decide which should be retained (could point to variety of types of evaluations)
- ☐ Fully examine and describe effective programs for duplication elsewhere (could point to process and outcomes evaluation)
- ☐ Other reason(s)?

Likely type(s) of evaluation to conduct:
Based on the purpose of the evaluation, what type(s) of evaluation is likely?

- ☐ Implementation evaluation?
- ☐ Goals-based evaluation?
- ☐ Process evaluation?
- ☐ Outcomes evaluation?
- ☐ Other(s)?

Planning Your Program Evaluation (Cont.)

Be sure to copy and complete this worksheet for each evaluation question.

Evaluation Questions and Data Collection

Evaluation question:

Information Needed to Answer Question	Data Collection Method(s) to Obtain Information	How Method Will Be Implemented in Cost-Effective, Timely Fashion

Planning Your Program Evaluation (Cont.)

If your evaluation plans include an evaluation question that is directly in regard to assessing extent of achievement toward desired outcomes, fill in this worksheet for each outcome. Be sure to copy and complete this worksheet for each outcome.

Outcome Measurement Framework

Outcome:

Outcome target:

Indicator(s)	Data Source	Data Collection Method

Planning Your Program Evaluation (Cont.)

How will the evaluation results be reported, including to whom?

Who should conduct the evaluation?

Are there any other considerations that you need to make to complete your program evaluation plans?

Appendix E: Basic Methods in Business Research

Planning Your Business Research

Information in this section, "Planning Your Business Research," was written by Andy Horsnell, partner in Authenticity Consulting, LLC. This information is included with his permission.

What is Business Research?

Good business research is about collecting the information you really need, when you need it, to answer important questions and make important business decisions. What is the key to doing good business research? To make the best use of your time, get the information you really need, and make the best business decision, consider the following key questions before doing your research:

1. Why am I doing this research? What am I trying to answer as a result of this research? How important a question is it?

2. When do I need to answer my question?

3. What information do I really need to answer my question?

4. Where or from whom can I get the information I really need?

5. What options do I have to collect that information?

6. What resources do I have to collect that information? Who or what can help me?

7. Considering the time, options, and resources I have, what is the best way for me to get the information I need?

8. What am I actually going to do and when?

If you do not consider these questions, you run the risk of wasting your time and money, getting the wrong information and bad answers, and making bad business decisions.

For a more detailed explanation of each of these research planning questions, work through this list.

1. **Why am I doing this research? What important decision am I trying to make?**
    Always have an important decision in mind when you are doing your research. You are too busy to waste time collecting information to help make a decision that is not vital to your business, or worse yet – collecting information with no purpose in mind. With a clear decision in mind, you will be able to keep your research focused.

2. **When do I need to make my decision?**
    Timing is everything in business. Having 60% of the questions answered in time to make your decision is better than having 100% of the answers after the deadline's passed. But on the other hand, if your important decision really can wait, there's no sense in rushing into things and acting on less information that you might have been able to get if you had taken your time. So you need to have a clear sense of when you need to make your important decision.

3. **What questions do I really need to answer to make my decision? What information do I really need to answer my questions?**

   This is where many people get lost in their research. What do you really need to know to be able to make your business decision? Do you need to know a little about a bunch of things, or a lot about a few things? What kind of information do you need? Numbers? Opinions? And how much is enough? (A good rule of thumb is, the more important the decision, the better the information you should collect.) How you answer these questions will have a big impact on where you are going to have to go to get your information, and how you are going to get it.

4. **Where is the best place (and who are the best people) to get the information I really need?**

   Overall, information sources can be broken down into two kinds: primary and secondary. Primary sources are those people and organizations in your marketplace, for example, your potential customers, suppliers, and competitors. Secondary sources are reports, articles, and statistics *about* the people in your marketplace. A comparison of these two sources follows:

A comparison of primary and secondary information sources

	Primary Sources	**Secondary Sources**
Examples	Your potential customers, competitors, and suppliers in the marketplace.	Articles, reports, books, and statistics (about your potential customers, competitors, and suppliers) in libraries, bookstores, and on the world wide web.
Strength	You get to ask and observe what you want.	The asking and observing has already been done, saving you time and money.
Weakness	Asking and observing may take a lot of time and money that you may not have.	The secondary sources that are available may not have asked the questions that you need answered. You have to take what has already been collected.

While there are exceptions, it is usually safe to start with your secondary sources, because the information's usually readily available at low or no cost. Once you have gotten what you can from the secondary sources, ask yourself the question, "Do I *really* need more information to make my decision?" If you really do, turn your attention to your primary information sources to get the last vital pieces of information you need. But often you can get what you really need from secondary sources.

The real challenge for you with secondary information sources is not having too little information. You will likely be faced with a large amount of information for any decision. The real challenge will be to selectively pick the best from what is available. And it is always a good idea to use *at least* two good sources of information for any decision, and to make sure that these different sources agree with each other.

If you have done things right up to this point, selecting your sources – primary and secondary – should not be too hard. You will know what decision you are trying to make and when you need to make it, and you will know what information you really need to make that decision. And if you can explain this to the reference librarian at your local library, they will get you pointed in the right direction. It is worth noting that many people go "researching" way before they really know what they are researching – and they waste a lot of time in the process.

5. **What options do I have to collect that information?**
   With secondary information sources, collection is straightforward. You go to the source (library, resource center or website) and ask for the information. With primary information sources, deciding upon the right method is a little more involved. When considering your options, always remember to keep your business decision, timing and the information you really need clearly in your mind. These will help you to make the best decision.

6. **What resources do I have to collect that information? Who or what can help me?**
   You are almost ready to go out and do your research. One final consideration is about the resources you have, or have access to. These resources can include:

   - The time you are willing to commit

   - Friends and family members who are willing and able to help you

   - The money you are willing and able to spend

   - Access to the internet, your trainer

   - Other resource people in your community like the reference librarian at your local library

7. **Given the time, options, and resources I have, what is the best way for me to get the information I need?**
   Now it is time to make a decision about how you are going to do your research. This is not so much a separate step as it is something that will emerge as you go through the earlier steps. Still, it is good to stop and think it through one last time before you move forward.

8. **What am I actually going to do and when?**
   Okay – it is time to commit to a plan of action. Create a business research action plan to collect your thoughts. (Some of the worksheets in Appendix D might be useful for this.)

Overview of Methods to Collect Information

Program planning and evaluation requires collecting information in a systematic fashion to make certain decisions. The table on the following page provides an overview of the major methods used for collecting information in business, whether for-profit or nonprofit.

Note that many of the methods might be conducted face-to-face or over the Internet.

Methods to Collect Information

Method	Overall Purpose	Advantages	Challenges
observation	to gather accurate information about how a program actually operates, particularly about processes	-view operations of a program as they are actually occurring -can adapt to events as they occur	-can be difficult to interpret observed behaviors -can be complex to categorize observations -can influence behaviors of program participants -can be expensive
documentation review	to get an impression of how program operates without interrupting the program; is from review of applications, finances, memos, minutes, etc.	-get comprehensive and historical information -does not interrupt program or client's routine in program -information already exists -few biases about information	-often takes much time -info may be incomplete -need to be quite clear about what looking for -not flexible means to get data; data restricted to what already exists
questionnaires, surveys, checklists	to quickly and/or easily get lots of information from people in a non-threatening way	-anonymity -inexpensive to administer -easy to compare and analyze -administer to many people -can get lots of data -samples already exist	-might not get careful feedback -wording can bias client's responses -are impersonal -in surveys, may need sampling expert - does not get full story
interviews	to fully understand someone's impressions or experiences, or learn more about their answers to questionnaires	-get full range and depth of information -develops relationship with client -can be flexible with client	-can take much time -can be hard to analyze and compare -can be costly -interviewer can bias client's responses
focus groups	explore a topic in depth through group discussion, e.g., about reactions to experience or suggestion, understanding common complaints, etc.; useful in evaluation and marketing	-quickly and reliably get common impressions -can be efficient way to get range and depth of information in short time -can convey key information about programs	-can be hard to analyze responses -need good facilitator for safety and closure -difficult to schedule six to eight people together
case studies	to fully understand or depict client's experiences in program; conduct comprehensive examination through cross comparison of cases	-fully depicts client's experience in program input, process and results -powerful means to portray program to outsiders	-usually quite time consuming to collect, organize and describe -represents depth of information, rather than breadth

Ethics: Information Release from Research Participants

If your market research or evaluation will include collecting information about people and/or reporting that information, including their names or agencies, you should first get permission from the participants to collect that information and use it in your various evaluation reports. Participants have the right to participate or not in the research or evaluation. Consequently, you must clearly communicate the intended research activities to the participants, including what information you will be collecting, how you will be collecting it and what you plan to do with that information. The best way to communicate the research activities, solicit their permission and verify their permission is through use of an informed consent form. Have participants review and sign the form. Following is a sample of an information release form.

Information Release Form

I voluntarily agree to participate in the evaluation of the [*name of program*].

I understand that this evaluation is being conducted by program staff to improve the XYZ program.

I understand that any identifiable information in regard to a) my name and/or agency name and b) the particulars about my goals and activities carried out by me in the XYZ program will *not* be mentioned by anyone outside the program, either verbally or in *any* publication now or in the future, without my express, written consent.

I understand that any identifiable information in regard to my name and/or agency name may be listed *only* in the evaluation report to the funder and will *not* be listed in any other future publication(s).

I understand that the evaluation methods which may involve me are:

1. Program staff's observations of me in the program and/or

2. My completion of evaluation questionnaire(s) and/or

3. My participation in a 30-60 minute interview.

I grant permission for the interview to be tape recorded and transcribed, and to be used only by program staff for analysis of interview data.

I grant permission for the evaluation data generated from the above methods to be published in an evaluation report to the funder.

_____

Research Participant

_____

Date

Guidelines to Conducting Observations

Observation can be one of the most useful forms of data collection during research. Researchers use their five major senses (eyes, ears, touch, taste and smell) to collect information about environments, activities and interactions (verbal and nonverbal). Researchers can identify the information and interpret it according to their own nature and needs. They can also adapt their observation as the program processes change. In some cases, they can actually experience the activities. However, observers can greatly influence the behavior of the research subjects, which can unduly influence the research results. Observation can also be quite costly because it can take up so much of the observer's time, both during the observations and later on when organizing, analyzing and interpreting the information.

Note that, to be very good at observation during research, you need training and practice to notice and accurately record what you need to notice. As with any other research methods, you need to notice information that addresses your research questions. The following information provides you the 20% of guidelines that will generate 80% of usefulness when conducting observation as a research method. The remaining 20% of usefulness might come from reading more about conducting observations and actually carrying them out yourself.

Preparations

1. **Have clear and established research questions to guide your research.**
    Research questions are the questions that you are trying to answer by conducting your research. Usually the clearer and more specific the questions, the more focus during your research. Remember that everything that occurs in the research environment is data for you. You want to collect the data that is most relevant to answering the research questions.

2. **Clarify if you will be an "outside" observer or an observer-participant.**
    It might be easier for you to retain objectivity if you are an outside participant. (You are not taking part in the activities under observation or you will participate in the activities along with the research subjects). However, as an observer-participant, you can also experience the program first-hand. In that case, it will be more of a challenge for you to focus on objectivity during data collection.

3. **Ideally, use more than one observer.**
    Then data collection includes more than one perspective and one set of tools. However, it is usually rare that an organization can afford two observers.

4. **Use tools to help you quickly record what you are noticing from your five senses.**
    This can speed up the data collection and also reminds you of what to notice. For example, use a checklist of possible behaviors that you might see and when you see that behavior during your observations, note them on the checklist. You could use audio and/or video recorders.

5. **Test audio and/or video recorders.**
    If you plan to use them, testing reduces the risk of technical disruptions.

6. **Think about categories of information that you will collect.**
    Knowing the categories will help you to quickly record and organize the information. The categories can be identified by looking at what is needed to answer the research questions.

For example, if the research question is "How can we improve the program?," then you will want to collect information about program activities and processes, what people complain about, any ideas to improve the program, etc. Some broad general categories that you might consider are about the research subjects' environment, how they come into the environment, what resources they use, what activities they undertake alone, what activities they undertake with each other, how the subjects leave the environment and actual results for subjects.

7.   **Practice use of your data collection tools.**
Practice before you actually go into the research environment assures smooth and effective data collection.

8.   **Be rested.**
It can be quite tiring to conduct observations as a data collection tool.

9.   **Do not plan for extended observation activities.**
For example, you might limit observations to an hour followed by a rest period.

10.   **Always get written permission from research subjects.**
They deserve to know that they are taking part in a research effort and how you plan to use the information you collect from them.

 Use the sample information release form in Appendix E.

11.   **Fully disclose your research to participants,**
Including the purpose of the research and the activities that you will be doing. Acquaint yourself to the research participants and them to you, as well. Explain what you will do with the research results and, especially, how the research will benefit the participants. Provide time for them to ask you questions.

12.   **Allocate clean-up time immediately after the observations.**
You will use this time to collect your notes, write down information that you remembered but did not record during the observations, and organize your notes. For clean-up time, allocate the same amount of time that you used for your observations. For example, if you observed for an hour, allocate an hour for clean-up.

During Observations

1.   **Be sure that you are located in a place where you can see and hear what you want to observe.**

2.   **Set up your data collection tools.**

3.   **Remember that you are the "eyes and ears" for the research effort.**
You will want to be as thorough as possible in noticing important information and recording it thoroughly.

4.   **Remind the research subjects of why you are in the room.**
Hopefully, you have talked to them beforehand and had each of them sign an information-release form.

5. **Begin collecting information.**
    Use all five senses. Do not rely on your memory. Write it down or capture it on the data collection tool, such as a recorder.

6. **Take note of anything that will help you organize information captured by tools.**
    For example, write down notes about when the recorders were started or stopped.

7. **Describe the environment,**
    Including the physical space, any major tools and equipment, etc.

8. **Describe the people,**
    Including their roles, relationships to each other and how they intend to interact with each other.

9. **Describe the activities,**
    Including what people do alone and with each other.

10. **Note what happened and what did not happen.**

11. **Include quotations to mark any statements made by research subjects.**

Immediately after Observations

Overall, ensure that your data is organized and coherent such that someone else could use them to get a clear impression of what the research subjects did.

1. **Clean up your notes.**
    Clarify any scratchings, ensure pages are numbered, fill out any notes that do not make sense, etc.

2. **Note any special circumstances,**
    For example, you felt very tired so your observations might not have been quite complete or accurate, etc.

3. **Describe any personal reflections on the experience,**
    For example, subjects were very active, they seemed inhibited by your being there, etc. What did you see or hear that led you to the results of your reflections?

Guidelines to Writing Questionnaires

Preparation

Before you start to design your questions, clearly articulate what problem or need is to be addressed. Review why you are doing the evaluation and what you hope to accomplish by it. This provides focus on what information you need and, ultimately, on what questions should be in the questionnaire.

The following guidelines are relevant, whether you are conducting your research by using questionnaires on hardcopy paper or via the Internet.

Directions to Respondents

1.   **Include a brief explanation of the purpose of the questionnaire.**

2.   **Include clear explanation of how to complete the questionnaire.**

3.   **Include directions about where to provide the completed questionnaire.**

4.   **Note conditions of confidentiality.**
     Indicate who will have access to the information for evaluation purposes and whether you plan to restrict other access to responses. (Note that you should not guarantee confidentiality about their answers. If a court sued you to see answers, you would not likely be able to stop access to this information. However, you can assure that you will make every reasonable attempt to protect access to the answers.)

Content of Questions

1.   **Ask about what you need to know.**
     Get information about the goals or ultimate questions you want to address by the evaluation.

2.   **Ask questions that the respondent should be able to answer.**
     Make sure that the respondents can reasonably be expected to know the answers.

3.   **Ask questions that the respondents want to answer.**
     If the questions are too private or silly, the respondents may lose interest in the questionnaire or lose faith in the process.

Wording of Questions

1.   **Will the respondent understand the wording?**
     For example, are you using any slang, cultural-specific or technical words?

2.   **Are any words so strong that they might lead a respondent to a certain answer?**
     Attempt to avoid use of strong adjectives with nouns in the questions, for example, "highly effective government," "prompt and reliable," etc.

3.   **Ensure you are asking one question at a time.**
     Try to avoid use of the word "and" in your question.

4.   **Avoid using "not" in your questions if you are asking yes/no questions.**
     Use of "not" can lead to double negatives and cause confusion.

5.   **If you use multiple-choice questions, be sure your choices are mutually exclusive and encompass the total range of answers.**
     Respondents should not be confused about whether two or more alternatives appear to mean the same thing. Respondents also should not have a clearly preferred answer that is not listed among the choices of an answer to the question.

Order of Questions

1.   **Be careful not to include so many questions that potential respondents are dissuaded from responding.**

2. **Engage respondents early in questionnaire to increase motivation to complete it.**
Start with fact-based questions and then go on to opinion-based questions. For example, ask people for demographic information about themselves and then go to questions about their opinions and perspectives. This gets respondents engaged in the questionnaire and relaxed, before encountering more challenging and reflective questions about their opinions. (Consider if they can complete the questionnaire anonymously; if so, indicate this on the form where you ask for their name.)

3. **Attempt to get respondents' commentary in addition to their ratings.**
For example, if the questionnaire asks respondents to choose an answer by circling an answer or provide a rating, ask them to provide commentary that explains their choices and provide sufficient space and time to accept commentary.

4. **Include a question to get respondents' impressions of the questionnaire itself.**
For example, ask them if the questionnaire was straightforward to complete ("yes" or "no"), and if not, to provide suggestions about how to improve the questionnaire.

5. **Pilot or test your questionnaire on a small group of clients or fellow staff.**
Ask them if the form and questions seemed straightforward. Carefully review the answers on the questionnaires. Does the information answer the evaluation questions or provide what you want to know about the program or its specific services? What else would you like to know?

6. **Finish the questionnaire.**
Finish the questionnaire according to results of the pilot. Put a date on the form so you can keep track of all future versions.

Guidelines to Conducting Interviews

Interviews are particularly useful for getting the story behind a participant's experiences. The interviewer can pursue in-depth information around a topic. Interviews may be useful as follow-up with certain respondents to questionnaires, to further investigate their responses.

Before you start to design your interview questions and process, clearly articulate to yourself what problem or need is to be addressed by using the information to be gathered by the interviews. This helps you keep clear focus on the intent of each question.

Much of the information herein was adapted from Michael Patton's book, *Qualitative Evaluation and Research Methods* (Sage Publications, 1990).

Preparation for Interview

1. **Choose a setting with little distraction.**
   Avoid loud lights or noise. Ensure the interviewee is comfortable (you might ask them if they are), etc. Often, they may feel more comfortable at their own places of work or homes. Keep in mind that it may be more difficult to control interruptions there.

2. **Explain the purpose of the interview.**

3. **Address terms of confidentiality.**
   Note any terms of confidentiality. (Be careful here. Rarely can you absolutely promise complete confidentiality. Courts may get access to information, in certain circumstances.) Explain who will get access to their answers and how their answers will be analyzed. If their comments are to be used as quotes, get their written permission to do so.

4. **Explain the format of the interview.**
   Explain the type of interview you are conducting and its nature. If you want the interviewee to ask questions, specify whether they should ask questions as they arise or wait until the end of the interview.

5. **Indicate how long the interview usually takes.**

6. **Tell them how to get in touch with you later if they want to.**

7. **Ask them if they have any questions before you get started with the interview.**

8. **Do not count on your memory to recall their answers.**
   Ask for permission to record the interview or bring along someone to take notes.

Types of Interviews

1. **Informal, conversational interview**
   No predetermined questions are asked, in order for the interviewer to remain as open and adaptable as possible to the interviewee's nature and priorities. During the interview, the interviewer "goes with the flow."

2.   **General interview guide approach**
     The interview guide approach is intended to ensure that the same general areas of information are collected from each interviewee. This provides more focus than the conversational approach, but still allows a degree of freedom and adaptability in getting information from the interviewee.

3.   **Standardized, open-ended interview**
     The same open-ended questions are asked to all interviewees (an open-ended question is where respondents are free to choose how to answer the question, i.e., they do not select "yes" or "no" or provide a numeric rating, etc.). This approach facilitates faster interviews that can be more easily analyzed and compared.

4.   **Closed, fixed-response interview**
     All interviewees are asked the same questions and asked to choose answers from among the same set of alternatives. This format is useful for those who are not practiced in interviewing.

Types of Topics in Questions

Patton notes six kinds of questions. A person can ask questions about:

- **Behaviors**
  Regarding what a person has done or is doing.

- **Opinions/values**
  Regarding what a person thinks about a topic.

- **Feelings**
  Regarding what a person feels about something. Note that respondents sometimes respond with "I think ..." so be careful to note that you are looking for feelings.

- **Knowledge**
  Regarding what a person knows about a topic.

- **Sensory**
  Regarding what a person has seen, touched, heard, tasted or smelled.

- **Background/demographics**
  Standard background questions, such as age, education, etc.

Note that the above questions can be asked in terms of past, present or future.

Sequence of Questions

1.   **Get the respondents involved in the interview as soon as possible**.

2.   **Before asking about controversial matters (such as feelings and conclusions), first ask about some facts.**
     With this approach, respondents can more easily engage in the interview while warming up to more personal matters.

3.   **Intersperse fact-based questions throughout the interview.**
      A long list of fact-based questions tends to leave a respondent disengaged.

4.   **Ask questions about the present before questions about the past or future.**
      It is usually easier for them to talk about the present and then work into the past or future.

5.   **The last questions might be to allow respondents to provide any other information they prefer to add and their impressions of the interview.**

Wording of Questions

1.   **Wording should be open-ended.**
      Respondents should be able to choose their own terms when answering questions.

2.   **Questions should be as neutral as possible.**
      Avoid wording that might influence answers, for example, evocative or judgmental words.

3.   **Questions should be asked one at a time.**

4.   **Questions should be worded clearly.**
      This includes knowing any terms particular to the program or the respondents' culture.

5.   **Be careful asking "why" questions.**
      This type of question infers a cause-effect relationship that may not truly exist. These questions may also cause respondents to feel defensive, that they have to justify their response, which may inhibit their responses to this and future questions.

Conducting the Interview

1.   **Occasionally verify the tape recorder (if used) is working.**

2.   **Ask one question at a time.**

3.   **Attempt to remain as neutral as possible.**
      Do not show strong emotional reactions to their responses. Patton suggests acting as if "you have heard it all before."

4.   **Encourage responses with occasional nods of the head, uh huh's, etc.**

5.   **Be careful about the appearance when note taking.**
      If you jump to take a note, it may appear as if you are surprised or quite pleased about an answer, which may influence answers to future questions.

6.   **Provide transition between major topics.**
      For example, "we have been talking about (some topic) and now I would like to move on to (another topic)."

7.   **Do not lose control of the interview.**
      This can occur when respondents stray to another topic, take so long to answer a question that time begins to run out, or even begin asking questions to the interviewer.

Immediately after Interview

1. **Verify if the tape recorder, if used, worked throughout the interview.**

2. **Make any notes on your written notes.**
    For example, clarify any fragments, ensure pages are numbered, fill out any notes that do not make sense, etc.

3. **Write down any observations made during the interview.**
    For example, where did the interview occur and when, was the respondent particularly nervous at any time? Were there any surprises during the interview? Did the tape recorder break?

Guidelines to Conducting Focus Groups

Focus groups are a powerful means to evaluate services, especially to test new ideas. Focus groups are interviews, but with six to 10 people at the same time in the same group. A person can get a great deal of information during a focus group session.

Preparing for Session

1. Identify the major objective of the session.

2. Carefully develop five to six questions (see below).

3. Plan your session (see below).

4. Call potential members to invite them to the session. Send them a follow-up invitation with a proposed agenda, session time and list of questions the group will discuss. Plan to provide a copy of the final session report to members and let them know that they will get the report.

5. About three days before the session, call each member to remind him or her to attend.

Developing Questions

1. **Ask yourself what problem will be addressed by the information.**
    For example, do you need to examine if a new service or idea will work, or to further understand how a program is failing?

2. **Develop five to six questions**.
    The meeting should last one to one and half hours. In this time, you can usually ask at most five to six questions.

3. **Focus groups are multiple interviews.**
    Many of the guidelines for conducting focus groups are similar to conducting interviews.

Planning the Session

1. **Scheduling**
    Sessions are usually one to one and half hours long. Over lunch seems to be a good time for others to find time to attend.

2. **Setting and refreshments**
    Hold sessions in a conference room or other setting with adequate air flow and lighting. Configure chairs so all members can see each other. Provide name tags for members, as well. Provide refreshments, especially boxed lunches if the session is held over lunch.

3. **Ground rules**
    It is critical that all members participate as much as possible, yet also to move along while generating useful information. Because the session is often a one-time occurrence, it is useful to have a few, short ground rules that sustain participation, yet do so with focus. Consider the following three ground rules: a) keep focused, b) maintain momentum and c) get closure on questions.

4.   **Agenda**
      Consider the following agenda: welcome, review of agenda, review of goal of the session, review of ground rules, introductions, questions and answers, wrap up.

5.   **Membership**
      Focus groups are usually conducted with six to 10 members who have some similar nature, for example, similar age group or status in a program. Select members who are likely to be participative and reflective. Attempt to select members who do not know each other.

6.   **Plan to record the session with either an audio or audio-video recorder.**
      Do not count on your memory. If recording is not practical, include a co-facilitator to take notes.

Facilitating the Session

1.   **Major goal of facilitation is collecting useful information to meet goal of session.**

2.   **Introduce yourself and the co-facilitator, if used.**

3.   **Explain the means to record the session.**

4.   **Verify that the tape recorder (or any recording device) is working throughout the session.**

5.   **Carry out (implement) the agenda.** (See "agenda" above.)

6.   **Carefully ask each question before that question is addressed by the group.**
      Allow the group a few minutes for each member to carefully record their answers. Then, facilitate discussion around the answers to each question, one at a time.

7.   **After each question is answered, carefully reflect back to all of them a summary of what you heard all of them say** (the note taker may do this).

8.   **Ensure even participation.**
      If one or two people are dominating the session, call on others. Consider using a round-table approach, including going in one direction around the table, giving each person a minute to answer the question. If the domination persists, note it to the group and ask for ideas about how the participation can be increased.

9.   **Close the session.**
      Tell members that they will receive a copy of the report generated from their answers, thank them for coming and adjourn the session.

Immediately after Session

1.   **Make any notes about the recording or flipcharts.**
      For example, clarify any marks, number pages or fill out any notes that do not make sense.

2.   **Write down any observations made during the session.**
      For example, where did the session occur and when, what was the nature of participation in the group? Were there any surprises during the session? Did the tape recorder break?

Guidelines to Completing Case Studies

Case studies are particularly useful in depicting a holistic portrayal of a client's experiences and results regarding a program. For example, to evaluate the effectiveness of a program's processes, including its strengths and weaknesses, evaluators might develop case studies on the program's successes and failures. Case studies are used to organize a wide range of information about a case and then analyze the information by seeking patterns and themes, and optionally by comparing with other cases. A case can be made of individuals, programs, or any unit, depending on what the program evaluators want to examine through in-depth analysis and comparison.

Developing a Case Study

1. **All data about the case is gathered.**
    For example, if the study is to highlight a program's failure with a client, data would be collected about the program, its processes and the client. Data could result from a combination of methods, including documentation (applications, histories, records, etc.), questionnaires, interviews and observation.

2. **Data is organized into an approach to highlight the focus of the study.**
    In our example, data in the case might be organized in a chronological order to portray how the client got into the program, went through the program and did not attain the desired outcomes.

3. **A case study narrative is developed.**
    The narrative is a highly readable story that integrates and summarizes key information around the focus of the case study. The narrative should be complete to the extent that it is the eyes and ears for an outside reader to understand what happened regarding the case. In our example, the narrative might include key demographic information about the client, phases in the program's process through which the client passed, any major differences noticed about that client during the process and maybe early indicators of failures and key quotes from the client.

4. **The narrative might be validated by review from program participants.**
    For example, the client for whom the program failed would read the narrative to ensure it fully depicted his or her experience and results.

5. **Case studies might be cross-compared to isolate any themes or patterns.**
    For example, various case studies about program failures might be compared to notice commonalities in these clients' experiences and how they went through the program. These commonalities might highlight where in the program the process needs to be strengthened.

Guidelines to Conducting Pilot Research (Test Market)

A pilot research project includes 1) carefully implementing a particular design of a system (program, product, service, etc.) in a real-world or carefully simulated environment to 2) learn about the accuracy, validity and/or reliability of the design system. Ideally, the learning occurs as a result of implementing a particular research design, including carefully identifying specific research questions, collecting and analyzing data, and coming to conclusions about the design of the system.

Thus, a pilot research project is essentially an evaluation effort. Thus, the nature of research used in a pilot research effort is the same as that used in a program evaluation.

An advantage of a pilot research effort is the effort can be carefully designed to resemble, as much as possible, the final environment of the final design of the system while, at the same time, providing ample opportunities for collecting useful information about the application of the design. Usually the application is a relatively low-risk environment in which the project can be carried out without major risk to research participants. Disadvantages of pilot research can be high costs to develop a simulated or carefully monitored, real-world environment, and the additional delay before the final design of the system is made available.

Like other research projects, the usefulness and focus of the pilot research project depend on the focus and clarity of the research questions – the questions that are to be answered by the research project.

Planning Your Pilot

You will need to think about the following considerations, which are common to designing other research efforts. For more information about each of the following questions, see the section, "Planning Your Program Evaluation."

1. **Before you begin the pilot, complete the design of the system as much as possible,**
    So that the pilot program resembles, as much as possible, what will probably be the complete and final design of the system. Be sure that you know what you did to design the system. Otherwise, your situation will be like that of having cooked a great meal, but you would not know how to make the same meal the same way again.

2. **Design your research methodology.**
    Because the nature of a pilot research project is similar to that of a program evaluation, you can consider a similar research design, including the steps to identify:

3. **Who are the audiences that need the results from the pilot research of the system?**

4. **What is the management decision(s) that must be made about the system?**

5. **What research questions must be answered to make the decision(s)?**

6. **What kinds of information are needed answer the research questions?**

7. **From what sources should the information be collected?**

8. **How can that information be collected in a timely and cost-effective fashion?** Pilot research might include a variety of data collection methods, such as observation, questionnaires, interviews and focus groups.

9. **How can that information be analyzed, interpreted and reported?**

10. **Who should do the research activities and when?**

11. **Use the conclusions and recommendations to improve the design of the system.**

Convenient Methods to Collect Information

Far too often, we think we know what our clients think and want because – "well, we just know." Wrong! Nonprofits cannot be successful if they do not continue to meet the needs of their clients. Period. There should be few activities as important as finding out what your clients want for products and services and finding out what they think of yours. Fortunately, nonprofits can use a variety of practical methods to gather feedback from clients.

The methods you choose and how you choose to use them depend on what type of feedback you want from clients, for example, to find out their needs in products and services, what they think about your products and services, etc.

1. **Employees**
   Your employees usually interact most with your customers. Ask them about products and services that customers are asking for. Ask employees what customer complaints they hear.

2. **Comment Cards**
   Provide brief, half-page comment cards on which clients can answer basic questions such as: Were you satisfied with our services? How could we provide the perfect services? Are there any services you would like to see that do not exist yet?

3. **Competition**
   What is your competition selling? Ask people who shop there or use their services. Many people do not notice sales or major items in stores. Start coaching those around you to notice what is going on with your competition.

4. **Customers**
   One of the best ways to find out what customers want is to ask them. Talk to them when they visit your facility or you visit theirs.

5. **Documentation and Records**
   Notice what customers are buying and not buying from you. If you already know what customers are buying, etc., is this written down somewhere? Recording it ensures that it is not forgotten, particularly during times of stress or when trying to train personnel to help.

6. **Focus Groups**
   Focus groups are usually six to 10 people whom you gather to get their impressions of a product or service or an idea.

7. **Surveys by Mail**
   You might hate answering these things, but plenty of people do not – and will fill out surveys especially if they get something in return. Promise them a discount if they return the completed form to your facility.

8. **Telephone Surveys**
   Hire summer students or part-time people for a few days every six months to do telephone surveys.

9. **Web sites**
   You can get a great deal of information just by "surfing" or visiting the Web sites of

competitors, potential collaborators and groups of people who might be your clients. The Web sites often include information about mission statements, products and services, and the overall market positioning of the organizations.

Major Sources of Trends Information about Nonprofits

A wide variety of information sources can be useful during an external analysis. For example:

1. Find out what trade journals publish information about the types of clients that your programs serve and/or how the programs might better serve those clients. Sign up for at least two of them.

2. Contact educators about nonprofits. Their job is to stay up-to-date on nonprofit matters. Take them to lunch and interview them.

3. Take a course on nonprofit management.

4. Attend conferences on nonprofit matters. You can find out about many of the conferences by contacting the organizations that assist nonprofits (a list is provided, above).

5. Contact nonprofit alliances and councils and ask where you can get information regarding trends in services similar to those provided by your nonprofit.

6. The planning office of the city or state (or province) often has a vast array of information about trends in the area.

7. Interview some funders and examine their annual reports. Funders often have a good understanding of community needs and what is being done to address the needs.

8. Program evaluations are some of the best forms of information about how your nonprofit and its programs are doing! Probably your most important stakeholders are your clients. Nonprofits should have clear impressions of clients' impressions of those programs.

9. Conduct your own market research. Market research is collecting information about "markets" or groups of potential clients whose needs might be met by your nonprofit's programs, now or in the future.

Major Sources of Market Research Information

The following list conveys some of the major sources that nonprofits can reference to get information about markets, clients, trends, etc. The way that you use the following sources depends on the purpose of the information that you are seeking, for example, to understand more about your clients, a certain industry, a certain market, market trends, competition, etc.

1. **Census Bureau (in the USA)**
   There is a vast amount of information available to you, and much of this is on-line at http://www.census.gov/ or call 301-763-INFO (4636).

Statistics Canada (in Canada)
There is a vast amount of information about Canadian society and commerce. Go to
http://www.statcan.ca/start.html

2. **Chamber of Commerce (in the USA)**
Get to know the people in your local office. Offices usually have a wealth of information
about localities, sources of networking, community resources to help your business, etc. Go
to http://www.uschamber.com/default.htm or call 202-659-6000.

Chamber of Commerce (in Canada)
Similar to Chambers in the USA. Go to http://www.chamber.ca/newpages/main.html

Board of Trade (in Canada)
Various cities in Canada have a Board of Trade, for example, the Toronto Board of Trade,
that supports local organizations by providing information and resources and also supporting
networking among members. Reference the Yellow Pages telephone directories in Canada.

3. **Department of Commerce (in the USA)**
The Department has offices in various regions across the country and publishes a wide range
of information about industries, products and services. Go to http://www.doc.gov/ or call
202-501-0666.

4. **Libraries**
One of the richest and most helpful sources of information is your local library! Let the
Librarian help you. For example, in the USA, see:

a) *Directory of Associations*

b) *Sales and Marketing Management* magazine

c) *American Statistics Index (ASI)*

d) *Encyclopedia Of Business Information Book*

e) *Standard & Poor's Industry Surveys and Consumer's Index*

5. **Trade and Professional Organizations**
Organizations often produce highly useful newsletters for members, along with services for
networking, answering questions, etc. For example, in the USA, you can start by contacting
the National Council of Nonprofit Associations. Go to http://www.ncna.org/ or call 202-
962-0322. Also, contact the United Way of America or Canada, both of which publish a
variety of directories for nonprofits. Go to http://national.unitedway.org/index.cfm for the
United Way America or to http://www.unitedway.ca/english/ for the United Way Canada.

6. **Trade Publications**
Publications are becoming much more useful as various trades become more specialized and
their expectations are increasing for timely and useful information. The type of trade
publication that will be useful to you depends on the nature of your product or service, for
example, health care, arts or education.

Analyzing and Interpreting Research Data

Often, when analyzing data, there are certain indications that seem to stand out right away from the data, for example, most program participants believe the program is very good or it is clear that the program seems confusing to most of your program staff. A primary goal in your analysis should be to notice all of the major indications. Usually this is not hard to do. Analyzing quantitative and qualitative data is often the topic of advanced research and evaluation methods. However, there are certain basics that can help you to make sense of reams of data.

 Those basics are described in the section of this Field Guide titled, "How Will You Analyze and Interpret Your Results," in Part III.

Appendix F:
Major Methods of Advertising and Promotions

There are a wide variety of methods to advertise and promote your organization and/or its programs. The following list comprises most of those major methods.

Collateral, Advertising and Outreach

Brochures or flyers

Many desktop publishing and word-processing software packages can produce highly attractive tri-fold (an 8.5 inch by 11-inch sheet folded in thirds) brochures. Brochures can contain a great deal of information if designed well, and are a common form of advertising.

 See the topic, "Writing Brochures," in our Free Management Library[SM] at http://www.managementhelp.org/commskls/brochure/brochure.htm.

Direct mail

Mail sent directly from you to your customers can be highly customized to suit their nature and needs. You may want to build a mailing list of your current and desired customers. Collect addresses from customers by noticing addresses on their checks, asking them to fill out information cards, etc. Keep the list on-line and up-to-date. Mailing lists can quickly become out-of-date. Notice mailings that get returned to you. Lists should be used carefully since they can incur substantial cost. You do not want to inundate your stakeholders with information so make the most of your message.

 See the topic, "Direct Mail," in our Free Management Library[SM] at http://www.managementhelp.org/ad_prmot/anchor429843.

E-mail messages

These can be wonderful means to getting the word out about your business. Customize your e-mail software to include a "signature line" at the end of each message. Many e-mail software packages will automatically attach this signature line to your e-mail, if you prefer.

 See the topic, "Netiquette," in our Free Management Library[SM] at http://www.managementhelp.org/commskls/netiquet/netiquet.htm.

Magazines

Magazine ads can get quite expensive. Find out if there's a magazine that focuses on your particular industry. If there is one, the magazine can be useful because it already focuses on your market and potential customers. Consider placing an ad or writing a short article for the magazine. Contact a reporter to introduce yourself. Reporters are often on the look out for new stories and sources from which to collect quotes.

See the topic, "Classifieds," in our Free Management Library^SM at
http://www.managementhelp.org/ad_prmot/anchor430093.

Major Newspapers

Almost everyone reads the local, major newspaper(s). You can get your business in the newspaper by placing ads, writing a letter to the editor or working with a reporter to get a story written about your business. Advertising can get quite expensive. Newspapers are often quite useful in giving advice about what and how to advertise. Know when to advertise – this depends on the buying habits of your customers.

See the topic, "Classifieds," in our Free Management Library^SM at
http://www.managementhelp.org/ad_prmot/anchor430093.

Neighborhood Newspapers

Ironically, these are often forgotten in lieu of major newspapers, yet the neighborhood newspapers are often closest to the interests of the organization's stakeholders.

See the topic, "Classifieds," in our Free Management Library^SM at
http://www.managementhelp.org/ad_prmot/anchor430093.

Newsletters

This can be powerful means to conveying the nature of your organization and its services. Consider using a consultant for the initial design and layout. Today's desktop publishing tools can generate interesting newsletters quite inexpensively.

See the topic, "Writing Newsletters," in our Free Management Library^SM at
http://www.managementhelp.org/commskls/nwslttrs/nwslttrs.htm.

On-line discussion groups and chat groups

As with e-mail, you can gain frequent exposure for yourself and your business by participating in on-line discussion groups and chat groups. Note, however, that many groups have strong ground rules against blatant advertising. When you join a group, always check with the moderator to understand what is appropriate.

See the topic, "Newsgroups," in our Free Management Library^SM at
http://www.managementhelp.org/gen_rsrc/newsgrps/newsgrps.htm.

Posters and bulletin boards

Posters can be powerful when placed where your customers will actually notice them. But think of how often you have actually noticed posters and bulletin boards yourself. Your best bet is to place the posters on bulletin boards and other places that your customers frequent, and always refresh your posters with new and colorful posters that will appear new to passers by. Note that some businesses and municipalities have regulations about the number and size of posters that can be placed in their areas.

Radio announcements

A major advantage of radio ads is they are usually cheaper than television ads, and many people still listen to the radio, either at work or when in their cars. Ads are usually sold on a package basis that considers the number of ads, the length of ads and when they are put on the air. A major consideration with radio ads is to get them placed at the times that your potential customers are listening to the radio.

 See the topic, "Advertising on Radio and T.V.," in our Free Management Library^{SM} at http://www.managementhelp.org/ad_prmot/anchor604248.

Telemarketing

The use of telemarketing is on the rise.

 See the topic, "Telemarketing," in our Free Management Library^{SM} at http://www.managementhelp.org/mrktng/telemrkt/telemrkt.htm.

Television ads

Many people do not even consider television ads because of the impression that the ads are quite expensive. They are more expensive than most major forms of advertising. However, with the increasing number of television networks and stations, businesses might find good deals for placing commercials or other forms of advertisements. Television ads usually are priced with considerations similar to radio ads, including the number of ads, the length of ads and when they are put on the air.

 See the topic, "Advertising on Radio and T.V.," in our Free Management Library^{SM} at http://www.managementhelp.org/ad_prmot/anchor604248.

Web pages

You probably would not have seen this on a list of advertising methods even two years ago. Now, advertising and promotions on the World Wide Web are almost commonplace. Businesses are developing Web pages sometimes just to appear up-to-date. Using the Web for advertising requires certain equipment and expertise, including access to a computer, an Internet service provider, buying or renting a Web site name, designing and installing the Web site graphics and other functions as needed (such as an on-line store for e-commerce), promoting the Web site (via various search engines, directories, etc.) and maintaining it.

 See the topic, "Building, Managing and Promoting Your Web Site," in our Free Management Library^{SM} at http://www.managementhelp.org/infomgnt/web/web.htm.

Yellow Pages

The Yellow Pages can be effective advertising if your ads are well-placed in the directory's categories of services, the name of your business is descriptive of your services or your ad stands out (for example, is bolded or in a large box on the page). The phone company will offer free advice about placing your ad in the Yellow Pages. They usually have packages for a combination of business phone line along with a certain number of ads.

Promotional Activities through the Media

Articles that you write

Is there something in your industry or market about which you have a strong impression or a significant experience? Consider writing an article for the local newspaper or a magazine. In your article, use the opportunity to describe what you are doing to address the issue through your business.

 See the topic, "Basic Writing Skills," in our Free Management Library^{SM} at http://www.managementhelp.org/commskls/anchor1589638.

Editorials and letters to the editor

Often, program providers are experts at their service and understanding a particular need in the community. Newspapers often take strong interest in information about these needs, so staff should regularly offer articles (of about 200 to 900 words) for publication.

 See the topic, "Managing Media Relations," in our Free Management Library^{SM} at http://www.managementhelp.org/pblc_rel/anchor1192381.

Press kits

This kit is handy when working with the media or training employees about working with the media. The kit usually includes information about your business, pictures, information about your products, commentary from happy customers, etc.

 See the topic, "Managing Media Relations," in our Free Management Library^{SM} at http://www.managementhelp.org/pblc_rel/anchor1192381.

Press releases or news alerts

They alert the press to a major event or accomplishment and request inclusion in the newspaper. They explain who, what, where, why and when. Some include pictures, quotes, etc., to make it easier for the reporter to develop an announcement or story.

 See the topic, "Managing Media Relations," in our Free Management Library^{SM} at http://www.managementhelp.org/pblc_rel/anchor1192381.

Public service announcements (PSAs)

Many radio and some television stations will provide public service announcements for nonprofit efforts. Usually, these PSAs are free.

Other Promotional Activities and Events

Annual reports

Disseminate these to key stakeholders; they are ripe with information if they include an overview of your year's activities, accomplishments, challenges and financial status.

 See the topic, "Annual Reports," in our Free Management Library^{SM} at http://www.managementhelp.org/finance/np_fnce/anchor1770427.

Collaboration or strategic restructuring

If your organization is undertaking these activities, celebrate it publicly.

 See the topic, "Organizational Alliances," in our Free Management Library^{SM} at http://www.managementhelp.org/org_ally/org_ally.htm.

Networking

Spread the word to peers, professional organizations and those with whom you interact outside the organizations, for example, educators, consultants, suppliers or clients.

 See the topic, "Networking," in our Free Management Library^{SM} at http://www.managementhelp.org/career/netwrkng.htm.

Novelties

It seems more common to find ads placed on pens and pencils, coffee cups, T-shirts, etc. These can be powerful means of advertising if indeed current and potential customers see the novelties. Consider whether you will incur additional costs to mail them.

Presentations

You are probably an expert at something. Find ways to give even short presentations, for example, at local seminars, Chamber of Commerce meetings, trade shows, conventions or seminars. It is amazing that a person can send out 500 brochures and be lucky to get 5 people who respond. Yet, you can give a presentation to 30 people and 15 of them may be very interested in staying in touch with you.

See the topic, "Presenting," in our Free Management Library[SM] at http://www.managementhelp.org/commskls/presntng/presntng.htm.

Relationships with key stakeholders

Identify at least one representative from each major stakeholder group and take them to lunch once a year. Short, informal exchanges that demonstrate concern can cultivate powerful relationships of interest.

Special events

These often attract attention, and can include, for example, an open house, granting a special award, or announcing a major program or service or campaign.

Special offers

We see these offers all the time. They include, for example, coupons, discounts, sweepstakes or sales. Consider offering them in association with special events, such as conferences or community events.

Recommended Readings – an Annotated List

The following readings are by no means all of the important works in each category. However, the listed works will provide you a strong start to understanding information in that particular category. Also, the bibliographies of many of the works listed below will help you to find related works from which you can continue to develop your knowledge about the particular category.

Boards of Directors

Building Better Boards, David A. Nadler (Editor), Jossey-Bass, 2005.

> This book describes how Boards can become high-performing teams. Lists the influences that have the greatest effects on Board success and principles to improve Boards. Although the book is based on research with organizations that have many resources, the principles still apply to small- and medium-sized nonprofits.

Exploring the Puzzle of Board Design: What's Your Type, David Renz, Nonprofit Quarterly, Winter 2004, Vol 11, Issue 4. (Also at http://www.nonprofitquarterly.org/section/655.html)

> The article reminds consultants that there is no one right design for Boards. The article clearly conveys the wide range of types, or personalities, of Board of Directors and how to categorize them. Includes a well-designed graph for discerning the type of any governing Board.

Field Guide to Developing and Operating Your Nonprofit Board of Directors, Carter McNamara, Authenticity Consulting, LLC, Minneapolis, MN, 2003.

> This guidebook explains how to start a Board and nonprofit organization, or to fix a struggling Board. It also explains all of the activities required for effective Board operations, such as staffing, meetings, decisions and self-evaluation.

The Strategic Board: The Step-by-Step Guide to High-Impact Governance, Mark Light, Wiley, 2001.

> Includes broad guidelines for achieving effective governance, such as establishing clear vision and values for strong leadership, effective delegation through clarity of roles and responsibilities, and translating Board decisions throughout the organization via clear management plans and measures.

Capacity Building

Building Capacity in Nonprofit Organizations, edited by Carol J. De Vita, Urban Institute Press, 2001.

> Written especially for foundations considering capacity building programs, but relevant to all providers. Depicts overall framework for nonprofit capacity building. Suggests eight aspects of effective capacity building programs and describes continuum of capacity building services. Free at
> http://www.urban.org/UploadedPDF/building_capacity.PDF

Building for Impact: The Future of Effectiveness for Nonprofits and Foundations, Grantmakers for Effective Organizations, 2002.

Report on the 2002 National Conference of grantmakers that highlights expected trends in philanthropy, suggesting more priority on nonprofit performance. Offers four possible scenarios that grantmakers might follow in the future. Challenges grantmakers to focus on their own organizational effectiveness for capacity building. Free at http://www.geofunders.org/_uploads/documents/live/conference%20report.pdf

Building the Capacity of Capacity Builders, Conservation Company, June 2003.

Provides overview of nonprofit capacity builders, suggests four key capacities for effective nonprofit organizations: leadership, adaptive, managerial and technical. Includes recommendations for capacity builders to improve services. Free at http: //www.tccgrp.com/pdfs/buildingthecapacityofcapacitybuilders.pdf

Echoes from the Field: Proven Capacity Building Principles for Nonprofits, Environmental Support Center and Innovation Network, Inc., 2002.

Suggests nine principles of effective capacity building. An excellent read for those who want to understand the broad context of capacity building and the realities of providing capacity building programs. Free at http://www.envsc.org/bestpractices.pdf

Effective Capacity Building in Nonprofit Organizations, Venture Philanthropy Partners, 2001.

Suggests seven overall elements of nonprofit capacity building. Describes lessons-learned from nonprofits that have engaged in successful capacity building efforts. Provides comprehensive assessment instrument to assess organizational effectiveness according to the seven elements. Free at http://vppartners.org/learning/reports/capacity/capacity.html

Lessons from the Street: Capacity Building and Replication, Milton S. Eisenhower Foundation.

Based on street-level experience from 1990 to 2000 in offering technical assistance and training for capacity building, especially with grassroots organizations in inner cities. Offers top ten lessons and recommendations for funders regarding assistance and replication of programs. Free at http://www.eisenhowerfoundation.org/aboutus/publications/lessons_intro.html

Mapping Nonprofit Capacity Builders: A Study by LaSalle University's Nonprofit Center, Kathryn Szabat and Laura Otten (1999?).

Overview of research to identify "the universe of capacity builders ..." Mentions capacity builders by general characteristics and reports results of research, with percentage of capacity builders in various categories. This is an interesting perusal for those wanting a quick impression of the world of capacity builders. Free at http://www.np-org-dev.com/survey.doc

Reflections on Capacity Building, The California Wellness Foundation.

Lists numerous lessons-learned from TCWF's implementation of capacity building services. Reflections and lessons-learned are numerous and meaningful for funders providing capacity building services. Free at http://www.tcwf.org/reflections/2001/april/index.htm

Results of an Inquiry into Capacity Building Programs for Nonprofits, by Susan Doherty and Stephen Meyer of Communities for Action.

Describes organizational capacity and why it is important. Explains why capacity building does not happen naturally and offers seven overall elements that work for capacity building efforts. Brief overviews of major areas of capacity building. Free at http://www.effectivecommunities.com/ECP_CapacityBuildingInquiry.pdf

Strengthening Nonprofit Organizations: A Funder's Guide to Capacity Building, by Carol Lukas, Amherst H. Wilder Foundation.

Describes types of capacity building services. Provides straightforward explanation of process for funders to consider offering capacity building programs and adds general strategic process for funders to identify which capacity building services to offer.

Financial planning

Bookkeeping Basics: What Every Nonprofit Bookkeeper Needs to Know, Debra L. Ruegg and Lisa M. Venkatrathnam, Amherst H. Wilder Foundation, 2003.

The book explains important practices and procedures in bookkeeping and the overall bookkeeping cycle, generating the most important nonprofit financial statements, and how to establish the most important financial controls in a nonprofit organization.

Streetsmart Financial Basics for Nonprofit Managers, Thomas A. McLaughlin, John Wiley and Sons, 1995.

The book describes how to make management decisions based on financial information. The book includes numerous, easy-to-reference diagrams, along with numerous examples. Includes on-line copies of useful checklists and worksheets.

Fundraising

Fundraising Basics: A Complete Guide, Second Edition, Barbara L. Ciconte and Jeanne Jacob, Jones and Bartlett, 2001.

This book explains the basics of fundraising, including critical foundations for successful fundraising, types of fundraising, how to plan your fundraising activities, and trends in fundraising. Includes fundraising on the Internet. Includes case studies and real-life examples.

Fundraising for Dummies, Second Edition, John Mutz and Katherine Murray, Jossey-Bass, 2000.

This book describes the most important basic considerations and activities to plan and conduct your fundraising. Includes how to get the Board engaged in fundraising, and how to research major donors and write grants. Similar to other *Dummies* books, this book includes a lot of handy tips and conventional wisdom.

Raise More Money: The Best of the Grassroots Fundraising Journal, Kim Klein and Stephanie Roth, Jossey-Bass, 2001.

This book combines the best advice from Klein's seminal publications on grassroots fundraising. The advice is always specific and easy-to-apply. This is a must-read for anyone working with small- to medium-sized nonprofit organizations. The advice still applies to nonprofits of any size.

Leadership and Supervision (includes staffing and volunteers)

Executive Director's Survival Guide, Mim Carlson and Margaret Donohoe, Jossey-Bass, 2003.

This book was written for the Chief Executive Officer who wants to understand all aspects of the role and develop into a wise and effective leader. Includes guidelines to avoid burnout, identify organizational effectiveness, lead organizational change and work effectively with the Board.

Executive Leadership in Nonprofit Organizations: New Strategies for Shaping Executive-Board Dynamics, Robert D. Herman and Richard D. Heimovics, Jossey-Bass, 1991.

The is one of the first publications to suggest that, although theory and law assert that the Board governs the organization, the quality of the working relationship between the Board and Chief Executive Officer is one of the most important determinants of the effectiveness of the organization.

Field Guide to Leadership and Supervision for Nonprofit Staff, Carter McNamara, Authenticity Consulting, LLC, Minneapolis, MN, 2002.

This guidebook provides complete, step-by-step guidelines to conduct the most essential activities in successful leadership and supervision in a nonprofit organization. Includes Board and staff roles, leading yourself, analyzing staff roles, recruiting and selecting staff, training and organizing staff, meeting management, performance management and how to avoid Founder's Syndrome.

Marketing (including advertising and promotions)

Successful Marketing Strategies For Nonprofit Organizations, Barry J. McLeish, Wiley, 1995.

The author argues that marketing is not just an activity, but should be an orientation among all management. Guidelines describe how to develop a strategic marketing plan from analyzing the external and internal environments of the nonprofit and then producing a plan that best fits both environments.

Workbook for Nonprofit Organizations: Volume 1 Develop the Plan, Gary J. Stern, Amherst H. Wilder Foundation, 1990

This book explains the theory and importance of marketing in nonprofits. It describes a five-step process to develop a marketing plan: establishing goals, positioning the nonprofit, doing a marketing audit, developing the plan, and associating a promotions campaign. Includes worksheets.

Program Evaluation

Evaluation of Capacity Building: Lessons from the Field, Deborah Linnell, Alliance for Nonprofit Management, 2003.

Describes results of research among a variety of capacity builders, along with descriptions of the general activities of each builder and what they are doing to evaluate their particular programs. Numerous lessons-learned are conveyed, as well as suggestions for further research.

Qualitative Evaluation and Research Methods, Michael Quinn Patton, Sage Publications, 1990.

Provides comprehensive overview of qualitative research and data collection methods, many of which can be used in practical approaches to market research and program evaluation.

Program Planning and Design

Designing and Planning Programs for Nonprofit and Government Organizations, Edward J. Pawlak, Robert D. Vinter, Jossey-Bass, 2004.

Books focuses on nonprofit and government organizations. Suggests step-by-step activities for major phases, including planning, implementation and program operations. Ideally suited to large organizations with complex programs and systems.

Strategic Planning

Field Guide to Nonprofit Strategic Planning and Facilitation, Carter McNamara, Authenticity Consulting, LLC, Minneapolis, Minnesota, 2003.

Comprehensive, step-by-step guidebook to facilitate a strategic plan that is relevant, realistic and flexible. Includes a variety of planning models that can be used and guidelines to select which model is best. Also includes on-line tools that can be downloaded for each planner.

Five Most Important Questions You Will Ever Ask About Your Nonprofit Organization: Participant's Workbook, Peter F. Drucker Foundation, Jossey-Bass Publishers, 1993.

Top-level workbook guides organizations through answering five key strategic questions: What is our business (mission)? Who is our customer? What does the customer consider value? What have been our results? What is our Plan?

Strategic Management: Formulation, Implementation, and Control, Fourth Edition, John A. Pearce II and Richard B. Robinson, Jr., Irwin Publishing, 1991.

Explains the strategic planning process in the overall context of strategic management. Explains complete strategic management cycle, primarily for large for-profit corporations. Much of the information applies to nonprofits, including processes that nonprofits tend not to do, but should.

Strategic Planning for Public and Nonprofit Organizations, John Bryson, Jossey-Bass Publishers, 1995.

Provides an extensive, well-organized and in-depth explanation of a 10-step strategic planning cycle that can be used in planning with organizations ranging from small to large. This book is often referred to as the seminal source of strategic planning expertise for nonprofit organizations.

Strategic Planning Workbook for Nonprofit Organizations, Revised and Updated, Bryan Barry, Wilder Foundation, St. Paul, MN, 1997 (651-642-4022).

Well-organized and readable, top-level workbook provides guidelines and worksheets to conduct strategic planning for a variety of types, sizes and designs of nonprofit and public organizations.

Systems Thinking, Chaos Theory and Tools

Chaos Theory Tamed, Garnett P. Williams, Taylor and Francis, 1997.

Intermediate-level, yet accessible, read on chaos theory, including the mathematical and physics backgrounds underlying its dynamics. Uninitiated reader might best be suited to first read "Complexity Theory and Organization Science" listed below.

Complexity Theory and Organization Science, A Journal of the Institute of Management, Anderson, Phillip, Sciences, 1999, v. 10, 3, May/June.

Explains core premises of chaos theory and how premises apply, especially to strategic management. Describes several strategic planning approaches that rapidly collect feedback from participants and can quickly adapt to feedback from external and internal environments.

Fifth Discipline, Peter Senge, Currency/Doubleday, 1990.

Senge's book is the seminal work in systems thinking and tools. It provides an understandable and cogent explanation of systems theory, its relevance to organizational and management development, and presents various tools to analyze and change systems.

Fifth Discipline Field Book, Peter Senge, et al, Currency/Doubleday, 1994.

This resource is rich with models, tools and techniques to analyze and change systems. The book is a compendium of resources contributed by various practitioners and is well designed for ease of reference.

Leadership and the New Science: Learning About Organization from an Orderly Universe, Margaret J. Wheatley, Berrett-Koehler, 1992.

This is a seminal work on self-organizing systems. Introduces the concept and explains how social and organizational systems resemble natural, biological systems. Self-organizing systems are major concept in understanding chaos theory.

Systems 1: An Introduction to Systems Thinking, Draper L. Kauffman, Jr., edited by Stephen. A. Carlton, from The Innovative Learning Series by Futures Systems, Inc., 1980, Stephen A. Carlton, Publisher, Minneapolis, MN, (612) 920-0060.

This handy booklet presents a concise overview of principles of systems thinking. The principles can be used to analyze systems and suggest approaches to successfully change systems, as well.

Index

Advertising and promotions..........................
   Also see Marketing
   assembling plans for 121, 122
   major methods of..................................237
   planning for...73
   resources to learn more about................246
   worksheet to plan for 193
Assessment of community needs 45
   worksheet for planning 163
Board of Directors
   in organization chart of the organization .12
   resources to learn more about................243
   roles in program management xi
   various committees involved in programs xi
Budgets..
   See Financial planning
Business plan
   assembling 125
   process of developing 29
   topics to consider to develop 29
Capacity building (resources to learn more
   about)..243
Collaborator analysis..................................64
   worksheet to do....................................182
Competitor analysis....................................63
   worksheet to do....................................180
Copyrights..
   See Intellectual property
Customer service..75
   worksheet to plan..................................195
Delivery of programs and services...............76
   worksheet to plan..................................196
Description of program 66
   worksheet to do....................................185
Financial planning......................................
   Also see Worksheets
   resources to learn more about................245
Financial planning for programs
   developing budgets during.......................80
   estimating program costs during..............68
   key terms in 80
   pricing analysis as part of 62
   sample program budget format for 87
   to operate programs 80
   worksheet to do pricing analysis in 178
   worksheet to do program budget in 206

Focus groups (conducting during market
   research) 229, 231
Fundraising 130
   assembling proposal for 130
   contents of plan 130
   knowledge required for effective 25
   proposal similar to good business plan....30
   resources to learn more about...............245
Goals..98
   identifying marketing 66
   SMART goals...22
Implementation evaluation ....
   See Program evaluation
Implementation of plans ....
   Also see Program planning, Plans
   capturing learning during 136
   tools to track status of..........................135
Intellectual property...................................65
   copyrights...65
   patents 65
   trademarks 65
Interviews (conducting during market
   research) 225
Laws and regulations
   to consider 65
   worksheet to identify relevant 183
Leadership
   resources to learn more about...............246
Leadership role in good programs 117
Life cycles
   considering in your organization.............18
   definition of..16
   various perspectives on 16
Logic models
   identifying preliminary...........................54
   worksheet to develop...........................173
Management
   and good marketing................................43
   approaches to good................................32
   resources to learn more about...............246

Market research...
    Also see Worksheets
    analyzing and interpreting results from.236
    basic methods to conduct.......................215
    completing case studies from 231
    conducting focus groups during 229
    conducting interviews during.................225
    conducting observations during............220
    conducting pilot research for.................231
    convenient, practical methods for..........233
    critical role of 43
    developing questionnaires for.................222
    ethical considerations during................219
    major sources of information..................234
    methods to do community assessments ...46
    overview of methods for........................217
    sources of trends regarding nonprofits ..234
    uses of...43
Marketing...
    Also see Advertising and promotions
    assembling plans for 121
    conducting analysis 56
    identifying goals for 66
    resources to learn more about................246
    worksheet to identify marketing goals...188
Markets ....
    Also see Marketing
    identifying benefits to each target 58
    identifying targets...................................56
    worksheet to identify targets, features and
        benefits..174
Materials for programs...............................78
    worksheet to plan..................................203
Mission
    definition of...34
    example of statement of.........................35
Naming and branding.................................60
    worksheet to do.....................................177
Nonprofit organizations
    free program to develop........................144
    mission, vision and values of...................8
    organization chart of medium to large.....13
    organization chart of small 12
    organization chart of start-up.................11
    organizations assisting...........................145
    sizes of...11
    sources of information about trends in ..234
    systems view of 7

Observations (conducting during market
    research)..220
Outcomes
    as type of evaluation.............................100
    identifying indicators for........................52
    identifying intermediate 50
    identifying long-term 50
    identifying methods to achieve 50
    identifying overall 49
    identifying short-term..............................50
    identifying targets for.............................52
    worksheet to identify.............................168
Outputs
    from systems 5
    identifying..54
Packaging 59
    worksheet to design..............................175
Patents..
    See Intellectual property
Planning..
    Also see Program planning, Plans
Plans
    action plans 37
    approving final version of....................134
    Business Plans.......................................125
    ensuring implementation of.....................21
    Fundraising Proposals 130
    having others review 133
    Marketing Plans 121
    Program Development Plans.................120
    Program Evaluation Plans.....................129
    Program Operations Plans.....................123
    Sales, Advertising and Promotions Plans
       122
    sections common to many.....................118
    Staffing Plans 124
Pricing analysis...62
    worksheet to do 178
Process evaluation ....
    See Program evaluation

Program evaluation ....
Also see Market research,
Also see Worksheets
analyzing and interpreting results from 109, 236
assembling plans for 129
basic ingredients for................................93
best methods to collect data during 107
best sources of data during 106
common types of 96
description of...92
ethical considerations during 112
goals-based as type of............................98
guidelines for successful........................24
identifying decisions to make from 103
identifying the audiences for 103
identifying what data is needed from.....106
identifying what questions to answer 105
implementation as type of......................96
major considerations to designing 94
myths about..91
outcomes as type of 100
pitfalls to avoid during..........................112
planning your...102
process as type of....................................97
reasons to do 92
reporting results of................................110
resources to learn more about................246
should you hire an evaluator? 102
testing plans for 111
understanding..91
who should conduct the 111
worksheet to plan..................................210
Program planning...
Also see Implementation of plans
basic process of.......................................20
build-it-and-they-will-come approach to .27
business development approach to 31
business planning approach to 29
chronology of activities in 41
common approaches to 27
ensuring successful 21
incremental approach to..........................29
key terms in 20
resources to learn more about................247
role of leadership during.......................117
seat-of-the-pants approach to..................28
worksheet to organize 189

Programs...
Also see Worksheets
common approaches to planning.............27
common configurations of 9
definition of...9
depicting systems of...............................14
developing budgets for...........................81
developing frameworks for 45
developing visions for.............................48
ensuring successful development of........24
estimating costs of..................................68
estimating costs of materials in 70
identifying desired outcomes for............49
identifying methods to serve participants 50
logic models of 14
planning development of........................68
planning for advertising and promotions in
....73
planning for customer service in 75
planning for delivery of services in.........76
planning for finances in..........................80
planning for materials in 78
planning for sales in 74
planning operations of............................73
sample program budget for.....................87
starting the..71
summary description of...........................66
typical types of services 10
versus activities 8
Questionnaires (developing for market
research) 222
Sales..74
assembling plans for..............................122
worksheet to plan 194
Staffing
assembling plans for..............................124
estimating costs of program 68
planning for...77
resources to learn more about................246
worksheet for planning..........................200
Strategic planning
all else flows from 34
description of...33
developing a basic plan during...............35
resources to learn more about................247

Systems ....
    Also see Systems view
    definition of *4*
    depicting program 14
    feedback with *5*
    goals of *6*
    inputs to *4*
    outcomes from *5*
    outputs from *5*
    processes in *5*
    resources to learn more about 247
    where direction comes from in 8
Systems view ....
    Also see Systems
    benefits of 3
    of nonprofit organizations 7
    of programs 14
    understanding of organizations and
        programs 4
Trademarks ....
    See Intellectual property
Unique value proposition 60
    worksheet to articulate 176
Vision
    definition of 34
    developing for program 48
    example of statement of 35

Worksheets
    for customer service planning 195
    for identifying program materials 203
    for planning sales 194
    for staffing planning 200
    how to download x
    to articulate unique value proposition ...176
    to develop logic models 173
    to develop vision for program 166
    to do a collaborator analysis 182
    to do a competitor analysis 180
    to do a pricing analysis 178
    to do community assessments 163
    to do description of program 185
    to do naming and branding 177
    to do packaging analysis 175
    to identify all marketing goals 188
    to identify outcomes for programs 168
    to identify program methods 170
    to identify program targets and indicators
     172
    to identify relevant laws and regulations
     183
    to identify target markets, features and
        benefits 174
    to list all advertising and promotions
        activities 193
    to plan delivery of programs and services
     196
    to plan program development 189
    to plan your program evaluation 210
    to prepare summary program budget 206

Notes

Additional Titles Specific to Nonprofits

Field Guide to Developing and Operating Your Nonprofit Board of Directors

In our experience, nonprofit Boards rarely struggle because they don't understand advanced concepts. Rather, Boards struggle because they haven't established all of the most critical, foundational processes to develop and operate a Board. This guide will help your Board establish those processes, whether you are just getting started or evolving to the next level of effectiveness. Comprehensive guidelines and materials are written in an easy-to-implement style, resulting in a highly practical resource that can be referenced at any time during the life of a Board and organization.

189 pp, comb-bound, 2003   Item #7110, ISBN 1-933719-01-X $30

Field Guide to Nonprofit Strategic Planning and Facilitation

The guide provides step-by-step instructions and worksheets to customize and implement a comprehensive nonprofit strategic plan – that is relevant, realistic and flexible for your nonprofit organization. The guide describes the most useful traditional and holistic approaches to strategic planning. It also includes the most important tools and techniques to facilitate strategic planning in an approach that ensures strong participation and ownership among all of the planners. Emphasis is as much on implementation and follow-through of the plan as on developing the plan document. Hardcopy and on-line worksheets help the reader to collect and organize all of the results of their planning process.

284 pp, comb-bound, 2003   Item #7120, ISBN 1-933719-02-8 $32

Field Guide to Leadership and Supervision for Nonprofit Staff

Top-level executives, middle managers and entry-level supervisors in nonprofit organizations need the "nuts and bolts" for carrying out effective leadership and supervision, particularly in organizations with limited resources. This guide includes topics often forgotten in nonprofit publications, including: time and stress management, staffing, organizing, team building, setting goals, giving feedback, avoiding Founder's Syndrome, and much more. It also includes guidelines to ensure a strong working relationship between the Chief Executive Officer and the Board.

204 pp, comb-bound, 2003   Item #7130, ISBN 1-933719-03-6 $30

Field Guide to Nonprofit Program Design, Marketing and Evaluation

Nonprofits have long needed a clear, concise – and completely practical – guidebook about all aspects of designing, marketing and evaluating nonprofit programs. Now they have such a resource. This guide can be used to evolve strategic goals into well-designed programs that are guaranteed to meet the needs of clients, develop credible nonprofit business plans and fundraising proposals, ensure focused and effective marketing, evaluate the effectiveness and efficiencies of current programs in delivery of services to clients, evaluate program performance against goals and outcomes, and understand how a program really works in order to improve or duplicate the program.

252 pp, softcover, 2003   Item #7170, ISBN 1-933719-08-7 $32

Field Guide to Consulting and Organizational Development With Nonprofits

This highly practical book combines the tools and techniques of the profession of Organization Development with the power of systems thinking and principles for successful change in nonprofits. The book also addresses many of the problems with traditional approaches to consulting and leading. The result is a proven, time-tested roadmap for consultants and leaders to accomplish significant change in nonprofits. You can use this book to accomplish change in small or large nonprofit organizations, for instance organizations that 1) have a variety of complex issues, 2) must ensure a strong foundation from which to develop further, 3) must evolve to the next life cycle, 4) need a complete "turnaround," 5) must address Founder's Syndrome or 6) want to achieve an exciting grand goal.

517 pp, softcover, 2005   Item #7180, ISBN 1-933719-00-1 $58

Additional Titles of General Interest

Field Guide to Leadership and Supervision in Business

Top-level executives, middle managers and entry-level supervisors in organizations need the "nuts and bolts" for carrying out effective leadership and supervision, particularly in organizations with limited resources. This guide includes topics often forgotten in trendy publications, including: time and stress management, staffing, organizing, team building, setting goals, giving feedback, and much more.

204 pp, comb-bound, 2002   Item #7430, ISBN 1-933719-23-0 $25

Authenticity Circles Program Developer's Guide

Step-by-step guidelines to design, build, manage and troubleshoot an Action Learning-based, peer coaching group program. The program can be used by consultants or an organization's leaders for training enrichment, problem solving, support and networking among peers.

127 pp, comb-bound, 2002   Item #7730, ISBN 1-933719-10-9 $25

Authenticity Circles Facilitator's Guide

This guide describes how to organize, facilitate and evaluate peer coaching groups. Groups can be facilitated by an external facilitator or groups can self-facilitate themselves. It can also be used to recruit, develop and support facilitators of peer coaching groups. The guide includes appendices with worksheets for the facilitator's use and a handy Facilitation Quick Reference tool.

114 pp, comb-bound, 2002   Item #7720, ISBN 1-933719-11-7 $20

Authenticity Circles Member's Guide and Journal

This guide provides step-by-step guidelines for group members to get the mos out of their Action Learning-based, peer coaching groups, including how to select goals to be coached on, how to get coached and how to coach others. The guide includes a journal of worksheets to capture the learning of the group members and a handy Coaching Quick Reference tool.

110 pp, comb-bound, 2004   Item #7710, ISBN 1-933719-12-5 $15

Coming in 2006 – Watch our website for news!

Field Guide to Developing and Operating Your Board of Directors

Field Guide to Strategic Planning and Facilitation

Field Guide to Leadership and Supervision in Business – Revised Edition!

To order

To get your copies of these and other useful publications, contact us:

Online: www.authenticityconsulting.com/pubs.htm

Phone: 800.971.2250 toll-free in North America or 1.763.971.8890 direct

Mail: Authenticity Consulting, LLC
                 4008 Lake Drive Avenue North
                 Minneapolis, MN 55422-1508 USA